D0941595

STAR-SPANGLED JETS

COMMUNITY LIBRARY CENTER
SAN LEANDRO CALIFORNIA

STAR-SPANGLED
JETS

J
358.4

The United States
Air Force Thunderbirds

P. L. Penney

Meredith Press   New York

Copyright © 1968 by P. L. Penney

All rights reserved. No part of this book in excess of five hundred words may be reproduced in any form without permission in writing from the publisher.

First edition

Library of Congress

Catalog Card Number: 68-18320

Manufactured in the United States of America for Meredith Press

Dedicated to the men of the United States Air Force Thunderbirds who have given their lives in the service of their country.

Foreword

The author would like to express her appreciation to every member and former member of the United States Air Force Thunderbirds who cooperated to make this book possible. Unfortunately, it would take several pages just to list their names—and no mere listing of names could possibly convey an idea of the assistance they rendered.

A special word of thanks, however, should go to the members of the staff of the Thunderbird Information Office, including Capt. Alan G. Schreihofer, First Lt. Steven K. Murata, and photographers Staff Sgt. Robert R. Ehlke and Airman First Class Robert Denham.

I would like to thank especially Joan Jensen, the Thunderbirds' secretary, whose efficiency and help were indispensable in the writing of this book.

P. L. Penney

Carmel, California

Contents

x

STAR-SPANGLED JETS

1

Jet Pilots Are People

The four silver jets streaked up, up, up into the cloudless blue sky in a sun-splashed diamond formation so tight they seemed to be huddling together to keep warm. In a sudden burst of trailing white smoke and engine roar, the formation split apart like an exploding skyrocket. With a flash and a twist, one plane was racing north, another south, one east, and one west. They rolled into a dive and plummeted down, down, down toward the earth.

Far below, the thousands of watching people sucked in their breath, then sighed, as the falling planes leveled off scant feet above the earth. Now they were rushing toward each other on a sure collision course and the crowd gasped again. The four planes crossed safely at midfield —as neatly stacked as pancakes on a platter.

The United States Air Force Thunderbirds precision aerial demonstration team had just completed another thrilling show.

Why?

If their purpose had been to entertain the thousands who gaped in wonder at the flying skill of these daring pilots, they had certainly achieved it. If they were trying to give the audience a spine-chilling experience, they had done that too. But these pilots were not stuntmen; they were members of the United States Air Force. Surely there was a deeper meaning behind the performance than simply entertainment or thrills.

Let's go back to the year 1953 and find out just what purpose the United States Government had in wanting a team of its airmen doing seemingly impossible aerial acrobatics.

In the early 1950's there was a new and awesome sound in the sky. The plane without a propeller—the jet—was screaming through the air at speeds very close to that of sound. While these strange craft had been in use with the Air Force for more than eight years, people still knew little about them except that they were very fast and very noisy. The Korean War had brought these speedy fighters and their pilots into sharp focus when the records showed the defeat of the Russian-built MIG by 14 to 1. The Jet Ace had become the new American hero; people looked upon him with wonder as a sort of superpilot.

"Why, you need three heads and six hands to fly those things," they declared.

It was when this "superpilot" idea began to invade the ranks of the fledgling airmen that the United States Air Force really became concerned. These young men, who were just learning to fly, watched the jets swooping through the sky and despaired of ever learning to master 25,000 pounds of metal and a cockpit full of complicated dials and switches.

Experienced veterans of the air knew better. "Anyone can do it with proper training," they insisted.

No one, however, was convinced—least of all those young birdmen.

Something had to be done.

Brig. Gen. Charles F. Born, commander of Luke Air Force Base near Phoenix, Arizona, was called to the Department of the Air Force Headquarters in Washington, D. C. There, when he reported to his superior officers at the Pentagon, he received some very strange orders. The high-ranking Air Force men at the very top of the department told him:

"We want you to select a team of your best pilots, organize them into a spectacular aerial demonstration act, and send them out on the road. They are to show people exactly what a well-trained pilot can do with a jet aircraft."

Then, not wanting the general to misunderstand, they added, "We don't want these men to do any fancy barnstorming tricks. Tell them to stick to the basic combat maneuvers we teach every fighter pilot in the Air Force. The audience at the shows these men will put on will be the American people who want to learn more about these jet planes, the young pilots who are so hesitant about taking these new, faster machines into the air, and our friends in other countries who are anxious to know our pilots and their aircraft. We have an important message for all of these, General, and we feel that an aerial demonstration team can say it best."

General Born returned to Luke Air Force Base and summoned Col. Levi Chase, who commanded Luke's Combat Crew Training Group. The General told the Colonel of his visit to the Pentagon and passed on the strange orders he had been given.

Colonel Chase had some of the finest pilots in the Air Force in his organization. It was their job, as instructor pilots, to teach the younger men to fly. The Colonel went back to his office and asked to see the records of all his instructor pilots. His first task was to find a man he could depend upon to lead this new team.

One name stood out above the rest—that of Maj. Dick Catledge. Catledge had entered the Air Force (then the Army Air Corps) as an aviation cadet in 1942. In a year he was flying combat missions in World War Two. On his twenty-third mission over Italy he was shot down and captured. Two weeks later he escaped and evaded the enemy for nine months. Here, indeed, was the man with just the right combination of courage and adventurous spirit needed to lead the new team.

Next Colonel Chase began searching for two men to fly the right- and left-wing positions. He needed a pair that could bring their planes in so close to Catledge's that they would seem to be touching. They must also match each other's maneuvers with perfect precision. What better choice than twins?

The Colonel just happened to have a set in Captains Buck and Bill Patillo, whose Air Force careers, like their features, were carbon copies of each other. The twins entered the service together as privates during World War Two, took their flight training together, and flew for the Eighth Air Force until Bill was shot down over Germany. The only time they were separated was the period during which Bill was a prisoner of war.

The new team was to fly the basic four-ship diamond formation, and a fourth pilot had to be chosen with great care. He would fly in the slot between the wingmen and snuggled under the tail of the lead ship. His position would be so close that if he raised the nose of his aircraft

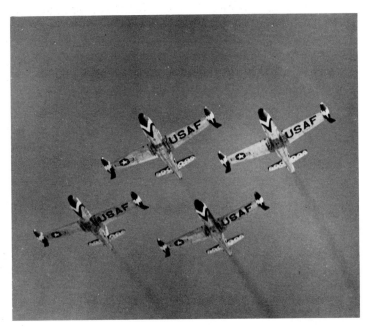

When the Thunderbirds were organized at Luke Air Force Base, Arizona, in 1953, they flew these red-white-and-blue F-84G Thunderjets. *Courtesy U.S. Air Force*

a few feet, the 3,000-degree blast from Catledge's jet exhaust would melt the canopy of his aircraft and him! Named for this job was Capt. Bob Kanaga, who had flown the P-47 Thunderbolt on Guam in World War Two and 105 missions in the F-86 jet in Korea.

Now the team was formed, but Colonel Chase added Maj. Robert "Mac" McCormick, who would learn all the positions so that he could fly as a spare pilot. Still not satisfied, the Colonel felt that one more pilot was needed. This man would serve as second spare and direct the maintenance of the planes. The choice was Lt. A. D. Brown, a man who knew jets inside and out, on the ground and in the air. He and Dick Catledge carefully picked fifteen of Luke's best maintenance men to keep the aircraft operating smoothly and safely.

The entire team was at last complete. There were six outstanding fighter pilots and fifteen of the finest enlisted men.

Then Colonel Chase and the pilots went into a huddle to select the jet fighter best suited to aerobatics. It had to be speedy, durable, stable in the air and easy to maintain on the ground. They agreed on the F-84G Thunderjet, a snub-nosed little fighter that had proved itself so well in Korea that it was used as the primary training plane at Luke in 1953.

Until now the group had been referred to simply as "the team." They needed a name. Everyone thought it ought to be truly American, and when someone suggested "Thunderbirds," it struck a happy chord.

They began to do some research into the name and discovered that it was certainly American—the Thunderbird was one of the most famous deities in Indian folklore. Many Indian nations believed the Thunderbird to be in control of almost all the powers man can imagine, but basically the idea of this god was that of good overcoming evil, of light over darkness.

The Indians believed the giant bird had the power to grant success in war and a long and honorable life. Such a great being was thus ranked with the Earthmaker, the Sun God, and the Chief of Eagles.

The physical appearance of the Thunderbird varied with each tribe, but it was usually pictured as a huge eagle or hawk. One illustration, crudely drawn by the Southwest Indians, pictured it in combinations of red, white, and blue.

The color scheme and the idea of an eagle, both symbols of their country, appealed to the team.

Indian legend attributed both thunder and lightning to these gigantic birds. Thunder was supposedly caused by the flapping of the bird's wings, while lightning was created by the blinking of the creature's eyes or sometimes by the arrows carried in its talons and hurled down to earth. Thunderstorms were said to be battles between the Thunderbird and rattlesnakes or predatory monsters.

The legendary thunder and lightning of the huge bird

and the very real roar and fiery blaze from the tailpipe of a modern jet fighter seemed a perfect simile. The name also fitted with the goodwill purpose of the team.

"It's everything we need in a symbol," the team decided. "From now on we'll be known as The Thunderbirds!"

2

On the Road

What sort of men were these new Thunderbirds?
The late J. H. Kindelberger, chairman of the board of
North American Aviation Corporation, gives us a vivid
picture of a jet pilot:
"At an altitude of about eight miles above the earth,
the pilot and his airplane are in a very thin and very cold
atmosphere. The temperature is about 60° below zero,
and the pressure is about two pounds per square inch, as
compared with almost fifteen pounds per square inch at
sea level. . . . Breathing free in this atmosphere, the pilot
could not remain conscious more than about thirty seconds and could not survive more than a few minutes. He
must be enclosed in a heated and pressurized compart-
ment, and he must have pure oxygen pushed into his
lungs under pressure. The thin air also handicaps the engine, to the extent that its effective thrust is barely
enough to win the fight against the weight and drag

This cutaway drawing of an **F-100** Super Sabre will give you an idea of the intricate machine that a Thunderbird pilot must maneuver through the air at near-supersonic speed. *Courtesy North American Aviation, Inc.*

of the airplane. Therefore the pilot must make every maneuver with delicate precision.

"Now let's take a look at the pilot. He finds himself packed into the sleek fuselage of a jet fighter with about a hundred controls to operate and twenty-four instruments to observe, plus a dozen indicators and warning lights to keep an eye on. In the fuselage with him is electrical and electronic gear equal in complexity to the combined circuits of a city power system, a radio broadcasting station, and the fire-control of a battleship. Under him and behind him run hydraulic lines, fuel lines, cooling and heating ducts, and oxygen lines. A few feet away is a giant blowtorch delivering as much effective power as three Diesel locomotives. And there he sits, loaded down with protective clothing, parachute, G suit, crash helmet, oxygen mask, and an acute bellyache caused by the expansion of his body gas at high altitude."

To this combination, the Thunderbirds added high-speed aerobatics, climbs, and dives that would take them from five to fifteen thousand feet within seconds, and planes flown so close that the wing tips overlapped three feet, with a vertical separation of only five feet!

So skilled was the new team that within a month of organization it was ready for a demonstration. It was decided to travel from Luke to Nellis Air Force Base, Nevada, three hundred miles to the north. Here their first show would be in the nature of a final examination after the hours of relentless practice. The men for whom they would perform were fighter pilots too. On June 1, 1953, the Thunderbirds flew a show at Nellis and passed the test.

It was the beginning of a rugged, exhausting summer during which the men worked fourteen hours a day. They flew their gaily painted red-white-and-blue jets with the star-spangled tails from Illinois to Colorado and from Florida to Texas. They appeared at air bases and Reserve Officer Training Corps camps and were applauded by men of the air who were familiar with every maneuver. They made their debut before the American people at the National Aircraft Show in Dayton, Ohio, and left the audience spellbound.

During a performance in Laredo, Texas, Lieutenant Brown learned just how costly a mistake can be to the symmetry of the show. He had replaced the vacationing Bill Patillo on right wing. With such a tight schedule of performances, he had only three days' practice.

After the show, Dick Catledge walked over and put a hand on Lieutenant Brown's shoulder. "You did a wonderful job, Brownie. Except, of course, for the . . . ah . . . slight error in the bomb burst."

"Yeah, I noticed." Lieutenant Brown's face turned a bright red. "What happened?"

"When you made your split-S and dove for the ground, you went to the left instead of the right. It looked okay to the audience, but it cost you in the crossover."

He had come out on the wrong side of the runway and was six hundred feet behind—or one half second off in the time schedule!

December arrived, and the Thunderbirds neared the end of their first season. As a climax, it was decided to fly a salute to the men who had really made it possible— Orville and Wilbur Wright.

On December 17, 1953, the nation prepared to celebrate the Golden Anniversary of powered flight. The day dawned cheerless, dull, and bitterly cold; yet thousands braved the blustering wind to stand on Kill Devil Hill in North Carolina where aviation had begun with the Wright Brothers' flight.

Soon the people watching forgot their discomfort. Four red-white-and-blue jets came streaking through the sky at six hundred miles an hour. The Thunderbirds skimmed in low across the base of the sand dune. They came in a string formation, single file. The whine of their engines became a roar. The day was shattered by a blast of power such as the Wright Brothers had never dreamed of. The gay markings of the planes were a sharp contrast to the billowing, slate-colored clouds. The crowd stood transfixed as the planes circled the limestone monument and screamed over the upturned faces burned raw by the gnawing wind.

The four jets climbed into the sky, dived toward the earth, and made the crossover in the famous bomb burst. As they roared away to the west, the cheers of the crowd were a fitting climax to the year of the Thunderbirds' beginning.

3

Wings over Sugar Loaf

*Los Thunderbirds de la Fuerza Aérea de los Estados Uni-
dos* means "the Thunderbirds of the United States Air
Force." The words were to become familiar to the team in
early 1954.

On January 15 the Thunderbirds flew to MacDill Air
Force Base near Tampa, Florida, where they joined a
goodwill task force that would take them on their first
tour out of the United States. The next month was spent
visiting Mexico, Nicaragua, Peru, Chile, Argentina, Brazil, Uruguay, Venezuela, Cuba, Panama, and the Domini-
can Republic. It might seem strange that such a trip
would be undertaken in the middle of winter until you
remember that much of the country through which they
would travel lies south of the equator. The warm and cold
seasons there are the reverse of ours. Christmas in Rio de
Janeiro is sometimes celebrated in a 100-degree heat
wave, while July may have freezing temperatures.

Although the team's mission was one of peace and goodwill, they were also demonstrating the long-range, precision striking capability of the United States Air Force. In order to show that they were ready for any emergency, the Thunderbirds carried a whole hangarload of spare parts in the giant cargo plane that went with them. They would be going to many countries where jet aircraft had never been seen before.

This kind of travel was a new experience that taxed the ingenuity of the maintenance men and the pilots. At one airfield they were to discover that, because there were no jets, there was no fuel for them. The maintenance chief used a mixture of 3 percent oil mixed with regular gasoline. Then, lacking mechanical equipment, the maintenance crew had to pump it into the aircraft by hand. They worked through the night. But morning dawned to find every plane fueled and ready.

One spot was so remote and wild that tigers were hunted just twenty minutes from the airfield, although the team didn't have time to try the sport.

A field booklet assuring the pilots that a smooth asphalt landing strip awaited them was wrong. They reached the field to find only a primitive dirt-and-gravel runway. They landed anyway. The gravel was thrown in every direction by the high-speed jets, and the planes were peppered with flying pebbles. Fortunately they came through this experience with only one broken windscreen. It was quickly repaired and off they flew.

When the Thunderbirds landed at the Mexico City airport, their first stop, they at once reminded that they were at a very high altitude, for it was hard to breathe. Mexico City is 7,800 feet above sea level, and in that rarefied atmosphere everyone has trouble getting enough oxygen—except the natives who are used to it.

Just before the show, the pilots were honored by one of the most ancient of Mexican customs. As they taxied their red-white-and-blue Thunderjets along the flightline on their way to take off for the performance, Mexicans jumped from the crowd and with bright capes made bull-fight passes at the wing tips. It was their way of showing appreciation for these fiery planes, as full of dash and bravado as any matador who ever faced a ferocious bull in Mexico City's Plaza de Toros.

A crowd of 300,000 jammed every available spot at the airport, while 1,200,000 more craned their necks from surrounding buildings to see Los Thunderbirds.

After Mexico, the team turned toward Central America, where their first stop was the tiny tropical country of Nicaragua. In all of its capital city of Managua there are only 65,000 inhabitants. It was said that 50,000 of them crowded the airport to watch the aerobatics of the team from the United States.

Traveling on a southeasterly course, the Thunderbirds next landed in the Canal Zone, from where they would fly over Panama City. Here, in the isthmus country where the Rocky Mountains seem to meet the Andes, the hills are only three hundred feet high and the distance from coast to coast is thirty-five miles as the crow flies, or, in this instance, as a Thunderbird flies.

Flying their show over the great canal, the pilots looked down to see huge ocean liners sailing slowly through the canal locks.

When they left this narrow neck of land behind them, the Thunderbirds turned south again, to take aerobatics down the West Coast of the continent of South America. The first stop was Lima, the capital of Peru and "City of Kings."

Although the Peruvians cling to the romance of their

past, their modern air force is one of the best in the world. After the Thunderbird show, the team stood proudly at attention to receive their wings as honorary pilots of the Peruvian Air Force.

Continuing their journey, they soared high over the vast desert in the north of Chile, then roared across the fertile middle zone and into the Aconcagua Valley to the modern city of Santiago, capital of the longest and narrowest country in the world.

After the show in Chile, the Thunderbirds turned east toward the city that once bore the very long name of Puerto de Nuestra Señora de Santa María de los Buenos Aires, but is known today simply as Buenos Aires, the capital of Argentina.

A few miles east of Buenos Aires is the city of Montevideo, the capital of Uruguay, the smallest nation in South America. It, too, saw a Thunderbird performance before the team continued north toward Brazil and Rio de Janeiro.

As a glance at the map shows, Brazil is the largest country in South America. Few people in the world know better how to enjoy life than the Cariocas, as the people of Rio are called. Great crowds of them pressed onto the white sands of Guanabara Bay at Rio de Janeiro to see the United States team. The sweeping shoreline of this loveliest harbor in the world is protected by two majestic mountain sentinels—the 2,310-foot Corcovado dominated by a gigantic stone statue of Christ, and Sugar Loaf, or Pão de Açúcar, which is only 1,300 feet high but still tall enough to rise over the somewhat less impressive peaks around the bay. The entire backdrop of moss-green hills gives the impression of a sleeping giant, with Sugar Loaf as the creature's bent knee. It was against these hills that the flashing red-white-and-blue Thunderbird jets spar-

kled in the sun of a Rio summer. They flew two shows—
one over the harbor and one over Copacabana, Brazil's
most famous beach resort.

The team had only three more places to visit when
they left Rio de Janeiro. Their next, and last, South
American stop was Maracay, Venezuela, where that country's fine military base provided an excellent point from
which the team's jets could take off and land. Not far
away is Venezuela's capital, Caracas—target for the performance.

Caracas lies three thousand feet high in the coastal
mountains that make a dark-green background for its
luxuriant gardens and red-roofed houses. It was here that
the hours of practice and the pilot skill of the Thunderbirds proved of great value. In the Bomb Burst, here
called *explosión de la bomba,* Bill Patillo looped and
dived toward the earth. The dive was made with the
sheer sides of 4,000-foot Mount Avila just a few hundred
feet below his flashing jet.

Leaving South America, the Thunderbirds flew over
the Caribbean to the group of islands called the Greater
Antilles. It was at Santo Domingo, capital of the Domini-
can Republic, that the Thunderbirds gave their show.

Their last stop in the month-long trip was the island
of Cuba. This, of course, was in 1954, before the rule of
Fidel Castro made a visit by the team impossible.

On February 14, 1954, the team and its task force landed
back at MacDill Air Force Base. They had flown eighteen
thousand miles and shown the jet aircraft in precision
aerobatics to millions of people. There were many new
friends in Central and South America because of *los
Thunderbirds de la Fuerza Aérea de los Estados Unidos.*

4

Practice Makes Perfect

"*There is no similarity between flying with the Thunder-*birds and with a fighter squadron. In Thunderbird flying, you constantly jockey the stick and throttle to stay in position. You get so that you sense you are about to move before you actually do."

The man speaking is a new Thunderbird. He has just come back from flying a practice show with the team and he is bone weary. His flying suit is soaked with sweat, and his eyes are still trying to adjust to the inside light after an hour or two of staring concentration in the fierce Nevada sun.

He chews thoughtfully on the stub of a pencil as we sit in the Thunderbird briefing room talking about those training sessions—the practice that makes the team perfect in the air shows. Anything less than perfection is intolerable for these experts.

"Stripped of its glamour, aerobatics is plain hard work,"

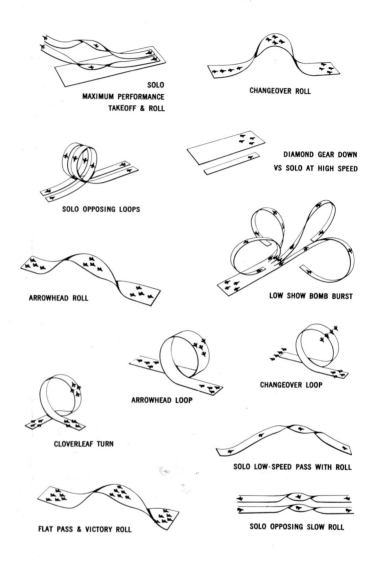

SOLO
MAXIMUM PERFORMANCE
TAKEOFF & ROLL

CHANGEOVER ROLL

SOLO OPPOSING LOOPS

DIAMOND GEAR DOWN
VS SOLO AT HIGH SPEED

ARROWHEAD ROLL

LOW SHOW BOMB BURST

ARROWHEAD LOOP

CHANGEOVER LOOP

CLOVERLEAF TURN

SOLO LOW-SPEED PASS WITH ROLL

FLAT PASS & VICTORY ROLL

SOLO OPPOSING SLOW ROLL

This diagram shows the present Thunderbird show sequence of aerobatic maneuvers. The demonstration changes from year to year as new maneuvers are added. Before a new "stunt" is adopted for the show, it is

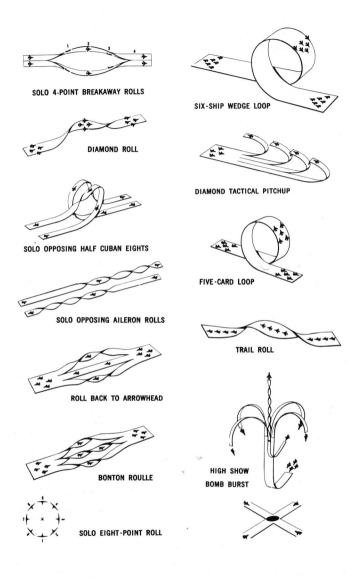

SOLO 4-POINT BREAKAWAY ROLLS

DIAMOND ROLL

SOLO OPPOSING HALF CUBAN EIGHTS

SOLO OPPOSING AILERON ROLLS

ROLL BACK TO ARROWHEAD

BONTON ROULLE

SOLO EIGHT-POINT ROLL

SIX-SHIP WEDGE LOOP

DIAMOND TACTICAL PITCHUP

FIVE-CARD LOOP

TRAIL ROLL

HIGH SHOW
BOMB BURST

first thoroughly tested on the practice range. *Courtesy North American Aviation, Inc.*

he says with a faint smile. "I love it, of course. I wanted to be a Thunderbird the first time I saw the team in action, and now it still seems like a dream. But when you're out there in the air learning to fly the show, you begin to realize that it's a lot different from anything you've done before.

"I was a fighter pilot with the 352nd Tactical Fighter Squadron out of Myrtle Beach in South Carolina before I was named to fly the right wing a few months ago. I figured I had a lot of experience and I was proud of the job I'd done. Before joining the team, I had crossed the the Atlantic twice and the Pacific once. I visited seventeen countries while flying my Super Sabre with the 352nd. It was rough flying. There were long hours in the cockpit when you felt that the only thing you wanted to see was that runway back at Myrtle. You got tired, but it still wasn't anything like this."

He paused to think back over those first days with the Thunderbirds, and I asked him to tell about his practice sessions from the very beginning.

"Did you start with the team, or did you practice your position until it was perfect before joining the others?"

"The former right wingman, the guy I was replacing, took me under his wing, so to speak." We laughed at the obvious pun. "He spent a lot of time with me. We sat around here playing with a couple of model Super Sabres like two boys playing games, but it was serious business for us. Those models weren't playthings. He was showing me some of the tricks he'd picked up in two years as right wingman with the Thunderbirds.

"Then we got into our flight suits and took the real aircraft on a practice mission. As we practiced the right-wing position, he showed me exactly how he'd done it. I watched and I listened. Even with all my experience as

These Thunderbird pilots are not playing games with toy airplanes!
Using models of the F-100 Super Sabre is one way in which a new pilot
can learn the maneuvering techniques of a Thunderbird demonstration. *Courtesy North American Aviation, Inc.*

a fighter pilot, I was pretty nervous during those first few practice sessions.

"After that first practice, I thought my arm would catch fire and explode from maintaining the forward pressure on the stick." He rubbed his arm—an indication that it was still protesting the increased use of muscles unaccustomed to aerobatics.

"The left wingman and I then flew three sessions in a two-ship formation, with my coach, the former right wingman, flying as chase pilot to keep an eye on my technique and my timing. Then we joined the leader and flew the three-ship formation. From this three-ship formation, we picked up the slot man and formed the diamond. Finally, the two solos came in and we began practicing the show sequence just as it would be done before an audience."

"Did you begin by practicing each maneuver until it was perfect?" I asked.

"No, from the very first practice flight we flew the complete show sequence each time. You memorize a few things and know the entire sequence before you go from the two- to the three-ship formation. Even after hours of practice, though, you know you can't fly flawlessly. There's never a lax moment."

This gave me an opportunity to ask about that first show before an audience. I'd heard it was the hardest show a Thunderbird would fly during his tour with the team. This man had flown his first show just a few days before at Nellis. The period for breaking in the new Thunderbirds was nearing an end. The team was even now preparing to take off for the next season.

"That first show *is* the worst!"

"Stage fright?"

"When you go out the first time before the public,"

he said, "your mouth is so dry it feels stuffed with cotton; your knees wobble and you're sure you'll forget everything you learned. Your hands begin to shake so badly that it's hard to buckle the straps of your parachute harness. And that's not the worst part of it! Out there in the audience are your parents and your kid brother, your wife and kids, and some of your buddies. By the time you climb into the cockpit, you're sure that you'll foul up. You don't, but they tell me that even after five or six shows I'll still have a touch of stage fright."

He pushed back his chair. "I have to check out my 'bird' now. I hope I've given you an idea of what our training is like. It's rough, but I wouldn't have missed this chance for a tour with the Thunderbirds. Aerobatic flying is a lot different, but it's really great."

This was the story of training from one of the new Thunderbirds; now I wanted to talk with the leader. It's his job to plan the training and lead the practice missions. The success of the team rests with the man in Thunderbird One, and it's in the practice sessions that he welds the team into a unified whole. Each man must blend his thinking into the concept of the team, but none more so than the leader.

He shoved aside the pile of papers on his desk as I entered. As leader of the team, he spends a lot of his non-flying time on paper work and in taking care of the details involved with traveling thousands of miles a year.

I asked him to describe the training procedure.

"In the first place," he began, "no new pilot could jump in and fly like a Thunderbird without practice, no matter how good he is. It takes five weeks of practice and about forty shows before he feels he has everything down perfectly.

"He begins at two thousand feet with the maneuvers

of the show sequence. When he's proficient, he comes down to the deck—about six feet off the ground. We don't have any minimum altitude, but we never get below thirty feet while flying a live show before an audience. I'd say a good bottom out at the end of a loop is about seventy feet.

"We train three new men a year now. It's naturally easier on the off years when the leader stays on. A new leader must learn the show sequence quickly and train his men at the same time."

He leaned back in his chair and folded his arms across his chest. The words came easily as he talked about the steps in training a man for the Thunderbirds.

"A new Thunderbird pilot is sharp in formation flying before he is accepted, so we don't need to go into the basics. There are, however, a few important differences in flying formation Thunderbird style. In the first place, the pilot undergoes a continual high g-force conditioning. He must learn to fly while fighting a nose-down trim, with those g-forces making it harder.

"Then, except for the flat pass and the Bomb Burst Crossover, the aircraft are constantly under stress. And there's the sun. A combat pilot uses the sun's glare as a weapon to help him surprise the enemy. If he flies into the sun, he's blinded. A pilot learning to fly combat becomes aware of the sun until positioning his plane in relation to it becomes a reflex. The Thunderbirds don't consider the sun. There is a definite line of flight. The team plays always with regard to the show center and the spectators. Sometimes a man must fly under a high-g condition, with nose-down trim, in turbulent air, and with the glaring sun in his eyes.

"These are some of the things he'll learn during the tour, but on the first practice the pilot concentrates on

Thunderbird diamond formation takes off. *Courtesy U.S. Air Force.*

alignment checks and how to stay just exactly where he is supposed to be. He practices rolls and loops with the Thunderbird's five-foot wing-tip clearance. He may be wide on his rolls and loops at first, but he learns the control technique and the trim procedures.

"On the second practice mission at Thunderbird Lake, the new pilot starts at two thousand feet and goes completely through the high show sequence including the Bomb Burst, Crossover, and landing practice pattern.

"It is vitally important for a Thunderbird pilot to know the show sequence by heart. If a diamond pilot loses radio contact during a show, the performance doesn't

Practice Makes Perfect

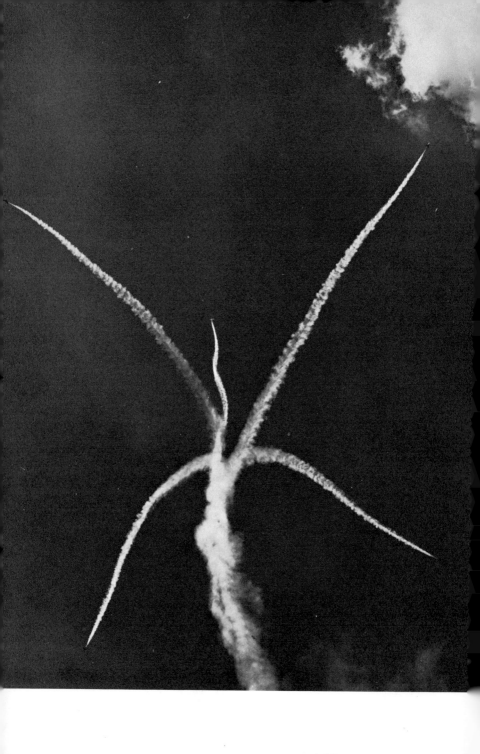

stop. He is so perfect that he knows exactly what to do and where to go. But he can't depend on instinct. It takes practice, practice, practice until he's letter-perfect in every maneuver."

He informed me that the minimum training period is a standard twenty missions, divided into three with the two-ship formation, three with the three-ship, six with the diamond, and eight with the solos making up the six-ship formation that has become a part of the show. "Usually," he said, "by the time the team is ready to open a season, we've managed to get in about thirty missions. Each one is the same—the show sequence, to get it committed to memory and, if there's enough fuel remaining, any specific maneuver we're having trouble with."

He leaned forward to pick up a mug of coffee. While he sipped the steaming brew, I asked about the sore arm the wingman had mentioned. He set the cup down and grinned.

"That's an occupational disease with new Thunderbirds. You see, we fly with nose-down trim. If we hit a bump in the air or the man in front wobbles, all we have to do to correct it is to relax our hand on the stick. It's smoother and safer. But the pilot is fighting this all the time he's flying. It can be compared with holding a twenty-pound bag of sand on your outstretched hand for thirty minutes." He held his arm out straight, with the palm up to demonstrate. "It's hard physical work at first, and a new Thunderbird is bound to come back with his arm aching. It takes many missions before a pilot's muscles are hardened."

The Thunderbirds break away to the four points of the compass in their renowned Bomb Burst, while a solo splits the center with vertical rolls. *Courtesy U.S. Air Force*

I asked what he considered the hardest maneuver for a new team member to master. He thought for a minute, as if silently measuring each maneuver against the other. Finally, he answered:

"The Bomb Burst is one of the trickiest maneuvers the team performs. For one thing, altitude can make a great deal of difference in the performance of the aircraft and in the efficiency of the jet engine. There is more thrust at sea level than at altitude. At a show in a place like Miami, Florida, the team goes from sea level to seven thousand feet in the Bomb Burst, but at the Air Force Academy at Colorado Springs they are already at six thousand feet before they start, and when they reach altitude for the Bomb Burst, they are at thirteen thousand feet!

"It can be calm near the ground and there can be sixty-knot winds at seven thousand feet. These are some of the variables the team must contend with and adjust for during the split-S and dive to the ground following the Bomb Burst—things a man must learn to handle with perfection. It demands the greatest amount of concentration and effort.

"The Crossover is the trickiest of all. In this maneuver the four Thunderbirds roar toward each other from the four points of the compass. The idea is to cross at midfield, with the planes neatly stacked one above the other at minimum altitude. We make a perfect cross perhaps once in every ten."

After the Crossover, the diamond re-forms and is joined by the solos in a six-ship formation. It appears to take place in a split second, and I asked how long the rejoin actually takes and how it is done so smoothly.

"The rejoin takes about a minute, but we try to make it appear so quickly that the audience is left wondering where we all came from. This means, of course, that we spend a lot of time and give special attention to the rejoin during our practice sessions. We have to pick up both solos and reform the diamond all in that sixty seconds of time. We keep talking to each other all during the Bomb Burst, Crossover, and rejoin. Each pilot makes minute adjustments in speed and position, depending on the radio information he receives from the others."

He went on to tell me that the practice sessions are held either at Thunderbird Lake or at Indian Springs Auxiliary Field. When the team moved from Luke to Nellis, Nevada, in 1956, Thunderbird Lake was turned over to them for practice. It's a huge dry lake ringed with mountains and set in the heart of the more than 3 1/2-million-acre bombing and gunnery range at Nellis.

Indian Springs is a tiny, jewellike Air Force base—a cluster of neat white buildings set in the vast brown desert about fifty miles northwest of Nellis. It has a runway and a forty-four-foot control tower. It is here that the Thunderbirds can practice in an area that closely resembles an actual show site.

The team must know what it is doing wrong during these practice sessions in order to perfect its movement in the air. A proper show critique involves more than pilots and planes; there are people behind the scenes who can, and do, contribute to the perfection of the show.

One of the pilots who has flown his last Thunderbird show and is staying to help break in the new members can be of invaluable help in criticizing a practice. The team photographer contributes hundreds of feet of movie film that can be studied over and over again. The narrator, whose job it is to present the show to the public, has a great deal of knowledge about the performance. He sees what the spectator will see—and more. The narrator is also a skilled pilot.

All of these people will climb the control tower at Indian Springs Air Force Base day after day to watch the team practice during the two-month standdown. The radio and tower communications experts keep constant control of all aircraft coming in and flying out of Indian Springs. When the Thunderbirds are practicing, it's the job of the controllers to keep other aircraft off the scene.

As the men inside the tower go about their job, the men who will criticize the show make their way to the catwalk where the cold winter wind cuts through heavy flight jackets and whistles past numbed ears and noses. A portable microphone gives them radio communication with the Thunderbirds, who will fly a complete show for these men to criticize.

Six tiny dots appear on the horizon to the south and west. The dots become red-white-and-blue Thunderbird Super Sabres coming in fast over the low mountain ranges ringing the tiny base. There is a flash of sun-splashed silver wings, and then the planes roar across the field with an ear-splitting burst of afterburner.

The practice is on. As they sweep across the field in the show sequence of rolls, loops, and whifferdills, the pilot whose job it is to criticize keeps up a lively commentary over the radio and directly into the cockpits of the six Thunderbird planes.

"Watch your alignment, Thunderbird Two. You were low on that last one."

"That loop was almost perfect. Beautiful, beautiful!"

Above the crescendo of noise created by the jets, the man's voice can be heard—now sharply critical, occasionally effervescent with praise, always helpful. If the loops and rolls are too wide, if the whifferdill takes too long, if the formation wobbles, that sharp, clear voice barks into the microphone.

A Thunderbird six-ship formation flying over Hoover Dam near their home base at Nellis. *Courtesy U.S. Air Force*

The narrator is there, too, with a clipboard and evaluation sheet. His pencil flies nearly as fast as the jets as he records each detail of the performance.

At the other end of the catwalk, the team photographer trains his movie camera on the planes. He is recording every move, good or bad, on film.

The Thunderbirds make their final six-ship pass and disappear into the distance—back over the mountains toward Nellis Air Force Base.

The three men climb down from their cold perch, pile into an Air Force car and start the fifty-mile drive back.

Practice Makes Perfect   35

It will take them at least an hour to cover the distance the team will fly in seconds.

Later, after the film has been developed, there will be a debriefing. Every flaw will be analyzed with clinical detachment. Each pilot will learn what mistakes he has made. There is nothing malicious in this criticism. No one, not even the leader, is spared the frank discussion on the day's performance. The debriefing is spiced sometimes with humor to help the men relax after the grueling practice. But it is pointed humor, and the laughter that follows is tempered with the knowledge that there's a lot more work ahead if the team is to achieve the perfection so important to the Thunderbird show.

There are millions of people waiting to see them perform. Each man must learn, in these few short weeks, to fly like a Thunderbird.

5

Whifferdills and Bomb Bursts

We've seen a jet pilot become a Thunderbird through hours of relentless practice. Timing, precision, and the show sequence have become second nature to him. Now let's travel with the team and see the end product of all this work—the actual demonstration.

Several thousand people are standing, sitting, or straining against the yards of rope that form a barrier between them and the six red-white-and-blue Air Force jets. Some of the more enterprising have found vantage points on rooftops, or even car tops; foresighted ones have brought camp stools, but they'll soon be on their feet craning their necks with the rest.

The ground crews make last-minute checks of the perfectly aligned F-100 Super Sabres standing like giant birds poised for flight. The people keep their eyes turned toward the aircraft. A hushed expectancy envelops the scene. Now a ripple of murmurs sweeps through the waiting crowd as six pilots appear in spotless white show suits with the Thunderbird emblem emblazoned on the breast pocket. The six men march smartly across the ramp toward the waiting planes. Each pilot is met by a click of heels and a snappy salute from his aircraft's crewman—the maintenance expert who cares for the F-100 like a baby.

The murmur grows to a restless hum.

The pilots climb steel ladders and settle into the cockpits. The crew chief of the lead aircraft, Thunderbird One, raises his right arm, the index finger of his hand extended. The other crew chiefs make the same signal: one minute to "start-engine" time. Soon these red-white-and-blue jets will lift into the air, their blazing afterburners providing a gigantic thrust of power. For thirty minutes they will zoom, dive, roll, loop, and twist through the air, changing position once every thirty seconds.

But before these Thunderbird pilots fly, they have work to do. Since no Thunderbird show has ever been canceled because of mechanical failure, the pilot knows his plane is in perfect condition. However, he's in business to get into the air safely and down in one piece, so he double-checks. Once in the cockpit, he has before him more than eighty separate buttons, gauges, dials, switches, hoses, and wires.

Because he is also a Thunderbird pilot, he has additional tasks before he starts that giant engine. He sees that the throttle and the master smoke switch are in the Off position. He sets the throttle and the emergency fuel selector, turns the master engine switch on, and waits for the signal from the leader's crew chief. The crew chief raises his hand to indicate Thunderbird One is ready to start, and the pilots turn their battery switches on. The chief salutes. A cloud of black smoke momentarily engulfs the planes as the pilots, in unison, depress the self-starter buttons and six Super Sabres pulse to life. Are they ready for takeoff? No, not yet. Each pilot puts the throttle in idle and watches the revolutions per minute start to build. Each monitors the fuel flow, sees that the ignition light is on, and that the tail-pipe temperature indicators light up. The rpm increases, and the pilot makes his final checks of gauges, switches, and dials.

The faces of the spectators show their excitement now as the hum of voices is replaced by the whine of the powerful jet engines. The crew chiefs remove the ladders from the sides of the aircraft and, on a signal from their flight chief, give the pilots a final salute; then they turn and march toward the crowd. Stopping twenty-five yards in front of the aircraft, the crewmen turn about and come to a "parade rest."

The pilots push their throttles forward and the engines respond with a louder whine. The lead aircraft begins to move, and the buzz of the watching people grows louder as they focus attention on the aircraft moving toward them. The leader turns sharply, and the other five Super Sabres fall in behind. They taxi toward the runway in close trail formation; only inches separating the nose of one aircraft from the tail pipe of the one in front.

They are lined up in a specific pattern that never varies. The leader is always Thunderbird One. The left wingman moves out as Thunderbird Two; the right wingman, Thunderbird Three; the slot man, on the right of Three, is Thunderbird Four. Immediately behind the diamond are the two solos as Thunderbirds Five and Six.

The whine of the jets fades as they move away; the crowd falls silent. The narrator steps before the microphone in front of the throng.

"Good afternoon, ladies and gentlemen. . . .

"To your left on the runway are the six F-100s that will perform for you today. As the pilots push their throttles forward, you will see black smoke pouring from the tail pipes as the F-100's engine develops its sixteen thousand pounds of thrust. With the engines at full power, the pilots will make their final checks determining that all systems are working perfectly...."

In the cockpits, the pilots are watching the rpm. It reaches maximum power and the voice of Thunderbird One comes over the radio. "Thunderbirds release brakes ... ready ... now!" Hands move in unison; another command, "Thunderbirds AB on ... ready ... now!"

A deafening roar splits the air. Fingers in the crowd point to the left. Flame shoots from four Super Sabre tail pipes as Thunderbird One calls, "Thunderbirds, one hundred and fifty knots ... nose gear off ... ready ... now!" As the flight breaks ground, Thunderbird Four slips smoothly into the slot position. The diamond turns and climbs in preparation for its first maneuver.

The eyes of the watchers dart to the left again. Thirty seconds after the diamond leaves the ground, Thunderbird Five gives a signal and the solos roll down the runway, gathering awesome speed. They break ground, climb steeply, and as one rolls to the right and the other to the left, the crowd gasps and hands clap in spontaneous applause.

The Thunderbirds are in the air!

What's it like to fly a Thunderbird show? To the watching audience, it looks as if the planes were floating through the air tied together. This illusion is so remarkable that a spectator was once heard to say to a friend, "One pilot flies one plane and his electronic stuff flies all them others." Another actually asked to see "the wires that hold the planes together."

The Thunderbirds operate their four ships in the in-trail or follow-the-leader formation as if they were a single airplane. *Courtesy U.S. Air Force*

But to a Thunderbird pilot it isn't nearly that easy. There aren't any wires or "electronic stuff" to keep the diamond in perfect formation. It's done by pilots who are using their heads, hands, and feet every second of that thirty minutes!

It isn't a matter of simply flying an airplane, either, but precision formation flying under varying conditions of body stress and strain.

For one thing, the air isn't the soft, smooth breeze we feel on our faces. The sky is full of holes and bumps and dips. If you've ever flown in an airliner, you probably have experienced the sinking feeling in the pit of your stomach as the plane struck an "air pocket" and dipped suddenly down like a ship in the trough of a wave. If you can picture that airplane flying with its wing tips over-lapping another by three feet and a vertical clearance be-tween them of about the length of a broomstick you'll get an idea of what the Thunderbirds experience.

Turbulence, as pilots call those air pockets, is only one of the problems a pilot faces in aerobatics. He keeps a positive pressure on the control stick at all times. Any relaxation of arm muscles will cause the nose of the air-craft to dip downward.

At the same time he's maintaining that stick pressure to keep the ship level, his body is undergoing intermittent high g-forces that increase his weight to two to five times normal.

While his right hand is clutching the stick, his left is working the throttle and his feet are busy on the rudder pedals. He guides, plays the throttle and rudders, jockeys for position to keep in formation, watches three other air-craft, operates the smoke switch, and keeps his eyes scanning the dials, gauges, and lights in the cockpit.

He does all of this at speeds up to 600 miles per hour, sometimes flying upside down or at right angles to the horizon, so that it appears vertical from the plane, keep-ing within a one-mile radius of the show area and changing position every half minute.

Let's follow the diamond now through some of its in-tricate maneuvers. Later, we'll fly with the solo pilots as they perform.

The diamond roars in toward the spectators for its opening pass at 400 miles an hour. As they pull up in front of the viewing area, trailing white smoke, they'll position for their first maneuver—the Cloverleaf Turn.

Thunderbird One calls for increased back pressure, and the pilots pull back on the stick. The aircraft nose up to a near-vertical position, then roll smoothly through a quarter circle and seemingly float over the top—inverted. Now they drop down the back side of the maneuver, with the speed increasing to pull out at 500 miles an hour directly in front of the audience.

The diamond has completed its first maneuver, but it must turn around quickly to be in the right spot for the next one. If they kept on flying straight and level, the Thunderbirds could easily make a half-circle turn and race back toward the audience, but it would take a lot of air space and a lot of time.

There's a far more graceful way to make a U-turn in a jet. The Thunderbirds call it a Whifferdill. Instead of going straight ahead, they pull the nose of the ship into a seventy-degree angle and make a 180-degree turn which sets them going in the opposite direction in about forty seconds. The graceful, elliptical U not only repositions them; it is another aerobatic maneuver for the benefit of the audience.

The loop has long been a favorite with men flying aerobatics. It's also useful to fighter pilots in combat. The Thunderbirds have incorporated the loop into many of their maneuvers. One of the trickiest of these is the Changeover Loop, which is entered in trail formation, with the planes shifting to come over the top in the diamond.

It starts with the four aircraft going into a follow the leader, or trail, formation, when Thunderbird One calls, "Changeover Loop is next."

The slot man's job is to position the Super Sabres one behind the other. He calls the signal, and the right wingman slides into position directly behind the leader. At the same time Thunderbird Two moves in behind him, while Thunderbird Four slips smoothly back to the rear of the trail.

The Thunderbirds are at the top of the loop. *Courtesy U.S. Air Force*

They skim through the sky like a train of cars with each pilot keeping the nose of his ship just below and perfectly aligned with the tail pipe of the aircraft in front.

Once again, the leader calls for smoke and then brings

the nose of his aircraft up to begin the climb into the loop. Before they "bottom" out in front of the audience, the diamond must be reformed while the pilots are undergoing a 4-g pressure. The trail climbs, and Thunderbird Three calls, "Thunderbirds change . . . ready . . . now." The wingmen break sharply right and left, and the slot man kicks in his afterburner to shove forward with a burst of power. Over the top they go—upside down and back in diamond formation. At the top, the diamond seems to stop in midair as Thunderbird One calls, "Relaxing the pull."

To the audience, it looks like magic, but it's all in knowing when to shift that fifteen tons of aircraft, in what direction, how far and how fast.

We've seen the diamond shift to a trail formation and back again; now let's see how the Thunderbirds' four aircraft resemble an Indian arrowhead. The right and left wingmen are going to drop back to fly formation on the slot man while they perform the Arrowhead Loop.

They need another Whifferdill to turn around, and as the leader stabilizes in his turn, Number Three calls, "Let's go Arrowhead . . . ready . . . now." The wingmen begin to drop back. In order to keep a safe distance above the slot man (whom they can't see), they'll fly slightly above the level of the leader's wings. As they catch sight of the slot man's Super Sabre, they shift to him as a point of reference and continue to drift back over his wings and down into position. The right wingman calls, "Three is in," to let the leader know he is free to maneuver.

Once again they're pulling a punishing 4-g force as they start through the loop. Reaching the top, they give the audience that extra thrill by slowing to minimum control speed. Then they start the long dive down, building up airspeed to 500 miles an hour.

Changing into a trail formation again, they come in for the Trail Roll that demands the utmost in smooth control technique on the part of each pilot. They'll keep the follow-the-leader formation in perfect alignment as they roll and pull through this maneuver. Any slight error could result in a crack-the-whip effect that would send the number-four aircraft careening to the outside of the roll—spoiling the precision and symmetry of the entire formation.

Rolling and looping in diamond formation is tricky enough, but the Thunderbirds can make it even tougher simply by adding one of the solo aircraft into the routine for a Five-Card Loop. In this one, they'll go up and over the top looking like the five-spot in a deck of cards.

What makes the Five-Card Loop so difficult? The swept wings of the Super Sabres are removed from the pilots' line of vision; yet they still maintain that minimum separation.

The right wingman comes forward to fly line abreast with the leader. The second solo races in to join the formation and fly line abreast with the left wingman. Right in the middle, completely surrounded by other aircraft, is the slot pilot, forming the fifth spot. They pull into the loop and go over the top looking just like the five of spades!

All over the world, men and women and boys and girls have thrilled to the spectacular finale of the Thunderbird performance—the famous Bomb Burst.

Even the narrator is more excited as he begins his description:

"The Thunderbirds are completing the Whifferdill turn and approaching at high speed still in their tight diamond formation. On the signal from the leader they will turn on their smoke and climb vertically. Having flown the entire show appearing to perform as one aircraft and separated by a scant few feet, the planes now approach the top of their climb for this maneuver, the Thunderbird Bomb Burst! The aircraft break away from each other to the four points of the compass, trailing white smoke much like a bursting rocket.

"Seconds ago the four aircraft were in tight diamond formation. Now, streaking away from each other, each will complete a half roll onto its back, dive through a split-S maneuver and straight down, pulling up at minimum altitude. Leveling off, the aircraft will fly directly toward each other and cross over at low altitude."

Ask a Thunderbird pilot about the Bomb Burst, and he'll surprise you by saying it's the first time in twenty-two minutes that he's had a chance to relax. He's all alone in the sky, without those other aircraft right on his wings. He can stretch his legs a little, check his fuel, feel free to move. It won't be long before the pilot will be right back in the thick of all those jets, but for a few moments at least, he and his "bird" have their own section of sky—all to themselves. This doesn't mean the Bomb Burst is easy. There's plenty to keep a Thunderbird busy.

The smoke goes on, and the Thunderbirds' F-100s come into vertical position, climbing almost straight up with the jets looking as if they were standing on their tails. The leader calls, "Thunderbirds, break . . . ready . . . now!"

The right wingman rolls 90 degrees to the right; the left wingman rolls 90 degrees to the left, and the slot man goes into a 180-degree rotation, while the leader continues into a loop.

And straight up through the middle of the formation comes the second solo, piercing the Bomb Burst with vertical rolls like a man following the trail of a corkscrew!

Boring into the sky and rolling away, the solo leaves just as the four ships execute a split-S maneuver in unison, yet hundreds of yards apart. Straight down they dive toward the earth to pull out just when it seems they must surely smash into the ground. Looks are deceiving, for each Thunderbird has perfect control over his ship.

The crossover is the really critical part of the maneuver. Each man, looping and rolling in an opposite direction from his opposing partner, must spot the other three planes as they begin to flatten out.

Now the four pilots, approaching each other from the four points of the compass at closing speeds of 1,200 miles per hour, must gauge distance, timing, and altitude while making minute corrections for wind, turbulence, and drift. Each pilot comes in slightly to the right of his partner and at a slightly different altitude.

Once again, the audience sees an illusion, for it looks as if the four ships were roaring straight toward each other on a sure collision course. They make the crossover at a predetermined point directly in front of the startled viewers—each plane stacked above the other.

As the four pilots complete the crossover, they maneuver to reform the diamond formation almost as quickly as it broke apart. The climax is over, but the Thunderbirds will streak by for one final pass, loop, and Victory Roll.

The solos join the diamond now for a six-ship wedge that loops in front of the audience. The wedge turns and enters once more to salute the audience with a giant Victory Roll—much like actors taking a final bow. As they come to the end of the show, the solos break away, and the diamond goes into its tactical pitchout and landing pattern. They slow their aircraft to landing-gear-lowering

Thunderbirds roar down in a six-ship wedge formation. *Courtesy U.S. Air Force*

speed, the gear goes down, the landing flaps are lowered, and they come skimming toward the runway at slightly more than 200 miles an hour. What keeps the plane from racing off the other end of the runway? As the wheels touch down, a giant red-white-and-blue drag chute pops from the rear of each Super Sabre. It acts as an extra brake, slowing the aircraft. The chutes are dropped, and the Thunderbirds roll gently to a stop and taxi into their parking space. Seconds later, the solos make their landing, and the narration stops. The show is over.

A group of children swarm around Captain Bob Beckel, number-one solo, seeking autographs after a show. *Courtesy U.S. Air Force*

As the six Super Sabres taxi back to the ramp, the spectators again strain at the rope barrier that holds them at a safe distance from the still whining engines. The whine stops; pilots climb down from their cockpits to be greeted by ringing applause. There is a short pause while the pilots post-flight-check their aircraft.

The barrier ropes are lowered and the crowd surges forward, with youngsters in the lead to get the pilots' autographs and perhaps have a memorable conversation with the six Thunderbirds.

This, then, is a Thunderbird demonstration—one of a hundred performed each year before a total of five million people.

As the Thunderbirds deploy throughout the United States and around the world to present their demonstrations, they represent the flexibility and rapid response of all units of the United States Air Force.

They are, however, a part of the Tactical Air Command. TAC, as it is more widely known, is the command in charge of the limited war force within the Air Force. With aircraft capable of carrying nuclear or non-nuclear weapons, TAC plays an important part in support of Army ground forces through its use of fighter, reconnaissance and assault aircraft. It is recognized as the most versatile and most mobile of all the Air Force commands. Under the direction of Air Force Headquarters, it organizes, equips, and trains the forces assigned to participate in tactical air operations.

With aerial refueling, today's tactical aircraft range has been increased at least fourfold over that of aircraft used during World War Two. It is really limited only by the endurance of the crew. The long-range mobility of tactical fighters is clearly demonstrated yearly by the non-stop jet flights of more than a thousand jet aircraft across the Atlantic.

It is from the ranks of these experienced fighter pilots that the Thunderbirds select their team members.

6

Upside-Down and Sideways

When the six red-white-and-blue jets roar down the run-
way to begin a Thunderbird demonstration and the narrator steps in front of the crowd to begin his description
of the show, he starts talking almost at once about the
solo pilots. It is these two men who open each performance. Their very first spine-tingling maneuver occurs on
take-off.

As the diamond formation completes its maximum per
formance climb and zooms away, the Thunderbird solo
pilots make their maximum performance climb in formation. At the peak of the climb and at minimum airspeed,
the solos roll their Super Sabres—one to the left, the
other to the right.

It takes the same skill, precision, and practice to fly
as a member of the duet of solo pilots as it does to fly in
foursome with the diamond. I talked with the lead solo
of the Thunderbirds. I wanted him to take me into the

The two Thunderbird solos in the Opposing Slow Roll on takeoff at a Thunderbird performance. *Courtesy U.S. Air Force*

cockpit in imagination at least. Here in the pilot's own words is a Thunderbird performance from the cockpit of the lead solo and his partner—better known as Thunderbirds Five and Six:

"The first thing we do, just like the boys of the diamond, is to check the cockpit. We have the same dials, switches, and gauges, and everything has to be working perfectly before we take to the air.

"We taxi out with the diamond and wait. When Thunderbird One says, 'Run 'em up,' the diamond pushes their engines to full military power, but we remain at idle. The diamond releases brakes and begins its takeoff roll. Forty-five seconds later we release our brakes and are off for the show!

"We roll down the runway at 150 knots, and when our speed reaches 160 we lift off and keep that speed indicator climbing to 180 knots and hold it there during the steep climb. Then we 'bleed off,' which means we allow our speed to drop back to 175 knots. I'm on the right and the second solo is on the left. I call, 'Turning and rolling,' and I make my takeoff roll to the right, while the second solo rolls left. We call it the Opposing Slow Roll on take-off, and it goes over big with the crowd.

"We have a landmark (a farmhouse, a railroad line, or a road) 14,400 feet out, which is our checkpoint. It must be exactly twenty seconds from show center, and at this point we adjust our airspeed so that when we come in for our maneuvers, we'll hit that show center on the dot. We do all our work at 425 knots indicated airspeed, or about 490 miles per hour.

"That first Opposing Slow Roll gives us a chance to check the drift and wind speed and to dress, or line up, on the show line, which is fifteen hundred feet in front of the audience. The second solo, Thunderbird Six, dresses on my aircraft.

"As we exit from the slow roll, we go into a Whifferdill to turn around for the Opposing Inverted Pass. We always make our turns behind the audience so that the people won't get interested in watching us and miss the diamond maneuvers. As the diamond makes its exit, we roar in from that twenty-second checkpoint to show center area for the Opposing Inverted Pass. We roll inverted

Thunderbird Six races to catch up with Thunderbird Five, which will give the illusion of a single ship passing the crowd. *Courtesy U.S. Air Force*

for the last fifteen hundred feet so that we pass the audience with both planes flying upside down."

I interrupted: "Is there a special trick to this upside-down flying?"

"Yes, there is: We throttle back our power to idle, which cuts down on the fuel flow and gives us exactly fifteen seconds of inverted flight."

In this pass the solos have passed each other, going in opposite directions. Now they must come in together for their next maneuver. After the pass, then, the lead solo goes into a Whifferdill to make his U-turn while the second solo races around behind the audience to catch up with him. Once again the diamond zooms away and the solos come in together for the Four-Point Roll.

Upside-Down and Sideways   55

The lead solo went on with his cockpit description.

"We turn the smoke on fifteen seconds from show center and gradually raise the noses of our Super Sabres to a five-to-seven-degree nose-high attitude.

"As I say, 'Nose coming up and one,' we turn 90 degrees. On the count of two we roll to 180 degrees or upside down, and on the count of three we're at a 270-degree angle or sideways, with the wings straight up and down, and at the instant I say, 'Four,' we roll back straight and level to go into our close formation and 'bug' out with our wings overlapping six feet.

"Our next maneuver is one of the most difficult we do. It's called the Calypso Pass, and much of it is done blindly, without either of us able to see the other. How I turn in this one can have a definite effect on the second solo. I make his work hard or easy.

"For this one, I call, 'Idle, ready ... now!' and roll inverted with as little movement as possible other than the turning of my aircraft. The second solo also comes to idle and drops his speed brakes for exactly one second to slow him down so that he won't overrun me. He comes in right side up, maintaining that six-foot wing overlap."

In order to give the crowd below the effect of blending fuselages, the first solo remains two to three feet below. This gives the proper angle to the audience.

The first solo went on, "I then roll out and right back in on the show, with a six-foot overlap to end the pass in formation. This rollback is the most critical point in the Calypso Pass. If I use too much forward stick, I'm liable to go right into or on top of Thunderbird Six. If he uses too much back pressure, it leaves him ahead and

The two solo pilots join "back to back" for their famous Calypso Pass. *Courtesy U.S. Air Force*

Upside-Down and Sideways

The two solo pilots roar toward each other for the Inverted-to-Inverted

we would have to re-form—giving the maneuver a sloppy appearance.

"I say, 'Break, ready, now,' and the second solo rolls 90 degrees to the left at lower altitude while I go straight up."

The diamond comes in for the In-Trail Roll, and Thunderbird Six positions himself to join them for the Five-Card Loop.

As the diamond exits, Thunderbird Five comes back for the Inverted-to-Inverted Pass. He uses the same entry as for inverted flight. At show center, he makes a complete 360-degree rollback to inverted flight for the exit.

maneuver. *Courtesy U.S. Air Force*

This is especially taxing because the nose of the aircraft wants to come down, and the pilot must keep it level with the horizon—while flying upside down!

Meanwhile, the second solo or Thunderbird Six has joined the diamond for the Five-Card Loop. He comes in behind the slot pilot until the formation is about halfway through the Whifferdill, when he comes in behind the right wing and lines up with the left wing. He must keep his tail just below the right wing's jet wash. As the diamond ends the Five-Card Loop and starts a left turn, the second solo says, "Six out," and breaks right. He goes into a Whifferdill for the familiar U-turn.

Upside-Down and Sideways 59

Continuing his cockpit description, the lead solo said, "I come back for the Eight-Point Roll with a stop every 45 degrees. By the time I reach show center, I'm making my 180-degree stop—halfway around or upside down. I measure my turns by using the horizon as my guide and measuring with my eyes. It would be impossible to fly this kind of a show on instruments."

The lead solo then goes into a Whifferdill for a U-turn while Thunderbird Six is ready for an approach from the opposite direction. The two will come toward each other and do a Half Cuban Eight. As they approach each other, the lead solo says, "Let's start 'em up, ready, now!" and they go into a 5-*g* pull going into the entry for the Half Cuban Eight. When they hit the vertical going up, they slack to 2 *g*'s. The pilots throw their heads back as far as possible to pick up the other pilot. "We talk our way through to pass with me about fifty feet above coming over the top."

To attain the illusion of passing nose to nose, they pull through to nose down 45 degrees and roll out simultaneously to a right-side-up position before each goes into a Whifferdill.

"The next maneuver is the Opposing Aileron Roll. I call it, 'Nose coming up and rolling.' We make four 360-degree rolls down to deck and back up into the Whifferdill.

"In the Opposing Loop, we again pull 5 *g*'s going into the vertical, slacken off to 2 *g*'s, and get a collision effect by trying to reach the vertical and bottoming out at the same time; then we exit in opposite directions."

The diamond comes in for a Cloverleaf while the second solo starts to position for the Bomb Burst. He trails the diamond about 2,000 to 3,000 feet as the team prepares for the Bomb Burst.

To keep the show moving while other planes are getting

ready, the lead solo comes in for a Wing Walk and Roll. Here's how:

"With the landing gear and flaps down in a landing configuration, I approach over the show line at 180 knots, rocking the wings 30 degrees to left and right. Just as I reach show center, I stop rocking the wings. Simultaneously I pull the nose abruptly up to about a 30-degree angle and light the afterburner when the aircraft hits a 45-degree angle. I then do a 360-degree roll, using a lot of forward pressure to unload the wing and make a cleaner roll. As I cut the AB, I make a turn out of the show area to position for the next maneuver."

On his heels is the diamond going into the famous Bomb Burst.

As the diamond goes in, Thunderbird Six is 2,000 feet higher and 2,000 feet behind, watching for the proper time to go up through the middle of the Bomb Burst.

As the diamond flattens out, Thunderbird Six goes down close in a steep dive, planing off at an altitude slightly higher than the diamond. He enters the maneuver at .94 Mach—just below the speed of sound, and starts playing his curve. With his higher air speed, he pulls about 7 g's to the diamond pilots' 3½–4 g's to get him into a vertical plane.

As the diamond goes into the vertical, he is two to three seconds behind to come through the Burst.

He comes out at the top of his climb, turns on his smoke and starts his rolls—he'll roar off rolling ten or twelve times as he does. In his rolls, Thunderbird Six pushes the stick to the left front corner of the cockpit and keeps his eyes on the airspeed indicator; if he looked out of the canopy while the ship is rolling, he'd get dizzy. He cuts the smoke, recovers from the rolls, and the plane "just about flies itself out."

Now the lead solo and the second solo come in to join

The lead solo begins his wing walk and roll down the runway during a show at Lakenheath, England, on the Thunderbirds' European tour in the Spring of 1967. *Courtesy U.S. Air Force*

the diamond in the last maneuver of the show—the Six-Ship-Diamond Wedge Roll and Flat Pass. The lead solo takes his position on the outside of the right wing and Thunderbird Six on the outside of the left wingman to form the six-ship wedge.

All six Thunderbirds come in for a roll, go into a Whifferdill, come back for a six-ship loop, and finally roll across the field with AB's screaming for a final Flat Pass.

The lead solo ended his description of the solo demonstration from the view in the cockpit. "We come in for the landing with a Calypso pitchout, with Thunderbird Six rolling out while I snap back underneath for my pitchup, landing right behind the diamond."

When you see the two solo pilots of the Thunderbirds flash by in a fantastic exhibition of rolls, passes, and loops, turning those Super Sabres every way but loose, it's hard to imagine a time when the lone solo pilot was so unimportant to the show that he sometimes never appeared at all.

But such was the case in 1954 when Ed "Lucky" Palmgren was a captain. He worked with Maj. Jacksel Broughton in the Bendix Trophy Race that year, and when Broughton took over as leader of the yearling Thunderbirds, he asked Palmgren to come along as solo.

"In the early days," Palmgren recalls, "the job didn't amount to much. A pilot usually flew the spot until a member of the four-ship diamond formation left. Then he took over whatever opening the departure created. As solo I'd come on and open the show with a few maneuvers to get the audience warmed up and give the diamond a chance to get in a little practice before they came in for the demonstration. After that, I landed and was just a bystander."

Palmgren decided the solo spot ought to have a little more dash, so he began to add to the routine. He added the vertical rolls and spin, often spinning his F-84F as many as seven times coming down in the dive after the vertical climb. He also added a low-altitude inverted pass with a snap into the air at the end and a four-point roll.

The six Thunderbird pilots make their last pass directly in front of the audience. *Courtesy U.S. Air Force*

"I began to make the solo's part real great—when I got the chance. But we only had five aircraft at the time. If something went wrong with one of the other four at the last minute, a diamond pilot would take my plane and leave me grounded."

The slot pilot left and Palmgren took his place, but he had established the solo routine as something more than the preliminary before the main bout.

While Palmgren was the first to make the solo's role important, it was Capt. John "Bart" Bartley who added the opening high-speed pass—and he did it quite by accident. The pass was dropped when the second solo was added, but the story of the high-speed opener with afterburner cutting in and out remains a Thunderbird legend.

It was at Daytona Beach, Florida, in 1957, and the Thunderbirds were about to begin their show before the several hundred thousand people who had come to see the famous annual auto races. The team leader, Major Broughton, looked down the stretch of long, curving beach over which the Thunderbirds were to fly. To his horror he saw that a flock of sea gulls had taken over and were soaring gracefully in the blue sky above. Everywhere he looked, he saw the black-tipped white wings of the big birds—hundreds of them. He knew what could happen if a gull was sucked into the intake of a jet engine. It could cause a crash; it might be fatal.

"Hey, Bart," he called to his solo pilot. "We're in trouble if those gulls don't take up residence somewhere else in a hurry. Fly down and see if you can scare 'em off."

Bartley took his jet into the air and came skimming over the sand, cutting his afterburner on and off. It sounded like a mortar battalion. The sea gulls flew off in a screaming cloud of white feathers, and the crowd applauded the performance enthusiastically. They thought it was a thriller put on for their benefit. As a result, the pass was kept as an opener for years afterward.

A few gulls once caused another solo pilot a great deal of trouble.

He was flying upside down when a gull came crashing through the canopy. At the same time another gull tore a hole in the fuselage. The pilot fortunately was able to flip his plane upright and land safely in spite of the unfortunate dead sea gull in the cockpit and the damage in the fuselage.

Upside-Down and Sideways 65

7

Halfway Around the World

The loudspeaker in the Military Air Transport terminal at Travis Air Force Base, California, crackled to life.

"Your attention, please. Flight 1158 is now loading at Gate Number 3 for immediate departure to Honolulu, Wake Island, and Okinawa. All aboard, please!"

Thirty-four men of the Thunderbird team grabbed suitcases and flight bags. The date was October 28, 1959, and the team was boarding a C-97 transport plane on the first leg of a whirlwind tour of the Far East that would take them to five countries.

Only that morning, the seven Thunderbird pilots, Major Robert Fitzgerald, Captains Charles Maultsby, Bob Janca, Neil Eddins, Gayle Williams, Herman Griffin, and the team narrator, Captain Dick Crane, had left their own sleek F-100 Super Sabres on the flight line at Nellis Air Force Base. These seven officers and the carefully selected ground crewmen who went with them would be gone fifty-five days. They were embarking on the most severe test of endurance, performance, and travel the team had faced in its seven-year history.

The Thunderbirds had thrilled millions in the United States, Central and South America, and Canada. Everywhere they went, people called them America's Ambassadors in Blue. It was a title not lightly given or received. Now it was felt that the people of Japan, Formosa, the Philippines, Korea, and Okinawa should have a chance to see the flashing jets.

General Emmett O'Donnell, Jr., commander in chief of the Pacific Air Forces, was later to write of the trip:

While the team's total contribution to the President's People-to-People Programs can never be accurately measured, be assured that their performance while on the tour, both in the air and on the ground, will stand as a monument to their own skill and to the mission which they were sent to perform.

Hundreds of words of praise were to follow the team on its route and a grateful Air Force was to honor it with one of aviation's highest awards.

But these things were in the future as the C-97 sped across the Pacific to its first stop at Hickam Air Force Base, Oahu, Hawaii.

The team would perform in seven standard F-100D first-line fighters borrowed from U.S. Fifth Air Force squadrons on Okinawa and Japan. Each airplane had to be thoroughly inspected and tested to make sure it was ready to become a Thunderbird plane. All of them had to be painted with the familiar red-white-and-blue markings. The tanks to hold the oil for the smoke had to be installed. When the Thunderbirds flew, they wanted to be sure that all the millions of people could follow each maneuver through the sky.

There could be no ifs, ands, or maybes. The planes *had* to be ready on November 11. The team and the crew of specialists landed at Kadena Air Base, Okinawa, on November 2. They went right to work.

"Anyone ever seen a typhoon?" asked Captain Griffin as they got off the plane.

"I sure have," came the prompt reply from one of the maintenance crew. "And, believe me, I ain't anxious to see another."

Captain Griffin eyed the sky with a mixture of dread and anticipation. He'd never seen one of the Far East's famous storms, but he didn't have long to wait.

The team was to experience two tropical storms before leaving the island and even "Griff" was to agree that more pleasant weather would be welcome.

Thanks to the excellent work of the weather observers at Kadena, they were prepared for the wild disturbance long before the winds and rains began drenching Okinawa with tons of water driven by savage gusts of wind. As soon as the typhoon alert was sounded, the Thunderbird maintenance men rushed to cover the F-100s and tie them down. The "birds" were safely buttoned up and suffered no damage, but the poor maintenance specialists were flooded in their barracks.

When the "all clear" sounded, signaling the end of the storm, the men looked sadly at the floor of the building they had been assigned to live in. There was water everywhere! Everyone grabbed a broom and began to sweep. They sloshed and swept and swept and sloshed and soon had the water and most of the mud outside again. Then they ran to the flight line. There was no time to waste. The Thunderbirds were scheduled to fly a practice mission.

As the pilots climbed into the clearing sky, Captain

Griffin looked off into the distance. There was the typhoon —still visible and dumping its gallons of water just a few miles away.

The second typhoon provided a wet welcome for thousands of Okinawan schoolchildren and their parents who came to watch one of the last performances of the Thunderbirds in the Ryukyu Islands. The inclement weather, the strange surroundings, even the rapid changes of climate failed to stop the Thunderbirds. It didn't even slow them down. They were ready on November 11. The day dawned with no sun. Flat, gray clouds scudded across the sky. A sharp wind tugged at the shivering Okinawans waiting to see the show. The team, however, wasn't going to disappoint these throngs, who had been standing in the cold for hours, and the performance went on.

Three days later, on November 14, they flew for the Kadena Air Base open house, made a quick trip to Itazuke, Japan, for a show there, and then back to Kadena for demonstrations to brighten the day for our own military men stationed on lonely outposts like Kune Shima in the Pacific. Then they were off in a burst of afterburner for the Philippines. Here, in just four short days, they flew five complete shows.

At Manila International Airport they joined in celebration of Philippine National Aviation Week. More than a million enthusiastic spectators gathered to watch the air forces of six nations in a four-hour show. A mighty cheer went up from the enthralled crowd as the Thunderbirds and their Philippine counterparts, the Blue Diamonds, blazed their white smoke trails across the sky to climax the day.

Then there was a rush to pack, make a last-minute

These Okinawan schoolchildren thrill to a Thunderbird performance at Kadena Air Base during the 1959 Far East tour. *Courtesy U.S. Air Force*

weather check, climb back into the Super Sabres, and take off for the next stop—the Republic of Free China.

The island of Taiwan (Formosa) lies just off the coast of China. It was here the forces of Free China under the leadership of Chiang Kai-shek sought refuge when the Communist Chinese gained control of their homeland. The people of Taiwan have a highly skilled air force.

Captain Griffin commented after his China visit, "I was particularly impressed with the Chinese Nationalist Air Force. I have only one thing to say about them. I'm glad they're on our side!"

The courteous, gracious Chinese were to award the Thunderbirds one of the highest honors they had ever received. To begin with, to show their appreciation for the opportunity of watching the performance, the Nationalist Government recessed its legislature early so the members and their staffs could watch the performance at Taipei.

This, in itself, was a tremendous compliment, but a wonderful surprise awaited the team when they landed and taxied back to park before the high-ranking government and military officials. The Thunderbird pilots stood in a very straight line while these important people walked by to shake hands and say, "We enjoyed the show. Your planes danced through the sky in a beautiful aerial ballet. Thank you so much for coming."

General Chen Chia-Shang, commander in chief of the Republic of Free China's Air Force, presented each pilot with the wings of a Chinese Air Force pilot. There was no doubt that America's aerial demonstration team had been truly accepted by their Chinese brothers of the sky, for these wings are never presented simply for ceremony —they have to be earned.

After a stay that seemed all too short, the team packed again. The next stop was like a homecoming for some of the men.

Many of the pilots and maintenance men were going back to Korea for the second time. The familiar sights and sounds of Seoul, Kimpo, Taegu, and Osan brought memories of the terrible wartime months they had spent in this divided country.

Sustained effort had begun to take its toll as the team finished its tour here, said good-bye to Korea, and turned east toward the Land of the Rising Sun. The tour was three quarters over, but the demands on the team had been tremendous. Pleas for "just one more show" had been heeded again and again, until the original ten scheduled shows had now been stretched to twenty-four. The men were tired.

Besides the grueling, energy-robbing performances, there had also been the pressure of personal appearances whenever the team was on the ground. A Thunderbird pilot, like a Hollywood star, must keep smiling even when he would much rather be back in bed at his hotel.

The ground crew, too, had borne heavy responsibility. There was the constant, painstaking maintenance performed under the worst possible conditions at strange air bases. There was the weight of meeting time schedules so critical that the pilots often flew a complete show, moved to another base, refueling by air en route, flew a second show, and only then landed their Super Sabres. Maintenance for this kind of flying had to be perfect.

The pilots and the men were exhausted physically and emotionally. It was now, in Japan, that the Thunderbirds —all of them—faced the "moment of truth." If the training, the discipline, the hours of practice, the *esprit de corps* were inadequate, the Thunderbirds would fail as a team and as America's Ambassadors in Blue.

Could the team meet this challenge? There was no hesitation. The pilots flew, parked their aircraft, lined up on the flight line, and smiled for their well-wishers. The ground crewmen took the precious planes and watched over them with tender care. Sagging spirits and tired bodies responded perfectly to the job at hand.

They flew five performances, four flybys, two practice air-refueling missions, and two photographic missions in just six days. At the end of it, they paused to look at the record.

The Thunderbirds had just flown twenty-nine shows in thirty-one days! It was the kind of flying that had never been equaled in the annals of aviation.

They had promised to fly two more shows in Hawaii on the way back to the United States mainland. Now, as they waited to get started on the journey home, the entire team began to think of Christmas with their families and friends.

But they couldn't just rush off across six thousand miles of Pacific Ocean without a good deal of preparation. Extra fuel tanks had to be hung on the thirsty fighters, survival gear had to be checked, advance crews had to fly ahead to meet the team at Guam and Wake Island. There were flight plans, briefings, weather checks, a thousand minute details—each important.

At last everything had been done and the Thunderbird pilots were ready for takeoff. Fitzgerald, Eddins, Janca, Maultsby, Griffin, Williams, and Crane would fly the seven Super Sabres to Hawaii with stops at Guam and Wake. The planes stood prepared to take off on December 15. The pilots awoke eager to begin their journey, but when they looked outdoors they knew there would be no takeoff that morning. Thick fog blanketed the runway. Anxiously they waited for the weather to clear. The next day, December 16, the front had moved on. There was a 2,500-foot ceiling, the air was crisp, and the sun glinted on the still-wet runways.

The heavy fighters taxied into position. The diamond, with Major Fitzgerald in the lead, would go first; followed by Griffin, Williams, and Crane in the remaining planes. The four-ship formation took off perfectly. The others waited, powerful jet engines screaming. It was then that Captain Crane saw a crew chief running toward him, flailing his arms wildly in an excited signal to stop. Crane cut his power. He could now see the fountain of fuel spurting from the left inboard tank. The cap was missing. As the jet whined to a stop, Crane called Williams, the leader of the three-ship formation. "Thunderbird Five, this is Thunderbird Seven. I've just blown a tank cap and am shutting down."

There was nothing to do but contact Fitzgerald and report that the flight would be delayed. Williams called the Major on his radio and told him what had happened. "We'll try to get off as soon as it's fixed."

Unless a replacement cap could be found immediately, the three planes would have to wait for many hours. There would be an entire new mission to plan before they could catch up with the rest of the team. It was a keen disappointment to the pilots who were longing to get home for the holidays.

The control tower could hold the flight plan open for only a very short time. There were many other planes waiting to take off from Yakota Air Base that day. A lengthy delay would throw everything into confusion.

The crew chief knew that there was no time to get a new cap from base supply. He jumped into a pickup truck, raced down the flight line, and braked to a halt in front of a B-66 bomber that he knew wasn't going anywhere that morning. Quickly the crewman unscrewed the cap from the gas tank, scribbled a note that said, "The Thunderbirds owe you one cap," left it where the crew would be sure to see it, and hopped back into the truck. He sped to Crane's waiting F-100. Captain Crane started his jet again. A few minutes later, three very happy pilots were winging through the sky.

In Hawaii, people from all over the island of Oahu flocked to Hickam Air Force Base to see performance Number 506, the last show of the Far East tour and the final one of the 1959 season. Just four days before Christmas, the Thunderbirds turned their Super Sabres east across the final miles of Pacific to Nellis and home.

They would refuel their jets from KB-50 tankers twice on the long flight. Getting fuel from these gas stations of the air is not quite as easy as pulling up to a gas pump at your neighborhood service station. It demands the utmost in precision and timing and coordination just to get the tankers and fighters together at the exact spot at the exact time. A missed rendezvous is very serious. The fiery jet engine of a fighter plane drinks vast quantities of fuel, and pilots can't afford to risk an empty tank over the ocean.

In order to accomplish the feat of meeting at just the right place, the tankers and fighters must use a special frequency on their radios as well as a homing system and radar. These particular refuelings occur at 20,000 feet, with all aircraft flying at a precise 210 knots per hour. This altitude and airspeed are particularly dangerous for the supersonic fighters. They are right on the edge of a stall.

A refueling probe juts out of the fighter plane's right

wing and extends nine feet into the air. The tanker carries a hose at the end of which is a large funnel called a drogue. The fighter pilot must fly his F-100 so that the probe is jammed right into the drogue. Then an amber light goes on in the tanker and fuel begins to flow into the fighter's tanks.

The hose reels out for sixty feet and once in the air it whips about and lashes at the fighter plane with the fury of an angry snake. Catching it isn't the easiest thing a pilot does. Once he has made contact, the fighter pilot flies in, pushing the hose back for thirty feet.

Once the F-100's tanks are filled, a green light goes on in the tanker. The fighter pilot backs off, climbs to his cruising altitude, and heaves a sigh of relief. Refueling is no fun!

Here is what Capt. Herman Griffin had to say about refueling thirsty Thunderbird fighter planes over the Pacific on the way home from Hawaii:

"Everything went according to Hoyle until our second refueling out of Hickam Air Force Base. We all got hooked up immediately, but the tankers had to fly into some very rough weather, and the hose began whipping about like a cork in a rough ocean.

"Two of the pilots were literally slung off their hoses and had to make another hookup. This could be compared to trying to drop a pebble into a swinging bucket from the top of the Empire State Building. Of course, when you're out in the middle of the ocean, it seems that your reflexes are working at their top performance. The two pilots managed to get rehooked and continued to get their full quota of fuel.

"I called for the tanker to reel out the hose to me and, lo and behold, the hose kept unreeling until it came completely off the tanker. I had to dodge it as it went by me and fell twenty thousand feet into the blue Pacific. That sort of shocked me a bit, as I had never seen that happen before."

In spite of the weather and the hose that never stopped unreeling, the seven Thunderbirds made the 2,700 mile flight from Oahu to Nellis in just 5 hours and 45 minutes. The final chapter in the Far East trip was written on May 15, 1960. The Thunderbirds stood stiffly and proudly at attention on the flight line at Andrews Air Force Base, Maryland. Gen. Thomas S. White, chief of staff of the entire United States Air Force, stepped down from the reviewing stand and walked toward them. Major Fitzgerald, Thunderbird leader, saluted smartly and then shook the General's outstretched hand. General White was there to present the team with the Mackay Trophy. This is one of aviation's most coveted honors and has been presented each year since 1912 to the person or organization making the most meritorious flight of the year for the U.S. Air Force.

For the Thunderbirds this truly said: MISSION ACCOMPLISHED!

8

The Plane Is Important

A first-line jet fighter aircraft was not designed to dance through the air with the grace of a ballerina. It is a heavy craft built for war, to seek out and destroy the enemy in the air or on the ground. A fighter is a functional plane. It can, and does, fly close formation in combat, but to do what the Thunderbirds make it do is alien to its nature.

However, the team was originally organized to fly the latest jet fighters in a spectacular demonstration of speed and maneuverability. This they accomplish. The fact that it's done in a plane produced for war and not for aerobatics makes their performance even more amazing.

The F-84G Thunderjet was the first aircraft chosen by the team for demonstration, partly because it was the hottest plane of the day and partly because most of the team was already very familiar with this little fighter. The fact that the name Thunderjet tied in nicely with the name Thunderbirds was coincidental.

The F-84G was a first cousin of the P-47 Thunderbolt —the famous "Jug" that had fought so effectively in World War Two. Manufactured by Republic Aviation Corporation, the Thunderjet was the first operational jet fighter to be equipped for midair refueling and the first to be designated by the Air Force to carry a nuclear bomb load. This combination of virtually unlimited range and devastating nuclear capability made it a very exciting airplane.

The Thunderjet had already proved itself in combat before the Thunderbirds made it gyrate through the air in precise maneuvers that left other fighter pilots gasping in disbelief. As the workhorse of the Korean War, the "G" earned the title "Champ of the Low-Level Bombers." It was said, in fact, that the Thunderjet was responsible for inflicting 60 percent of the fighter-bomber damage while comprising only 40 percent of the aircraft strength in Korea.

The "G" was a straight-wing ship that offered great stability and control and precise close-wing formation. Its wing span reached 38 feet from wing-tip tank to wing-tip tank. It was 38 feet long and 12 feet high, and the Allison J-34-A-29 engine developed 5,600 pounds of thrust, sending it scooting through the air at more than 600 miles an hour. It made the Thunderbirds the fastest aerobatic team in the world.

For a year and a half the team cavorted about the skies of North, Central, and South America, thrilling more than ten million spectators. They flew 130 shows and traveled 300,000 air miles in the Thunderjets. But the F-84G was becoming a rather old warhorse. It was time for a change. The Air Force had adopted bigger and faster jets. It was the job of the Thunderbirds to fly them in aerial demonstration.

In 1955 the team made the transition into the speedier, swept-wing F-84F Thunderstreak, which they flew for a year. *Courtesy U.S. Air Force*

Many veteran pilots shook their heads when it was announced that the Thunderbirds had selected the F-84F as the new demonstration plane. The "F" model, or Thunderstreak, was a "younger sister" of the F-84G, but there was one tremendous difference—the wings and tail of the Thunderstreak were swept back at a 40-degree angle.

These sweptwings were bound to make aerobatics more difficult, while stability problems were sure to increase as the Thunderbirds approached the speed of sound in the bigger and faster jets. But, while other pilots were skeptical, the team never doubted that the shiny new Thunderstreaks, fresh from Republic's Long Island factory, would take perfectly to their aerobatic role.

The F-84F wasn't a newcomer to the aviation world

when the Thunderbirds began to fly it. It had already claimed a new speed record for the Bendix race by flying 1,900 miles at an average top speed of 616 miles an hour. By making a flight from Los Angeles to New York in 3 hours and 44 minutes, it had set a new transcontinental speed record of 652 miles an hour. A flight of 5,118 miles from London, England, to Austin, Texas, had given the Thunderstreak the world's nonstop jet fighter distance record.

This was the plane that would carry the Thunderbirds from Portland, Maine, to Portland, Oregon; from the provinces of Canada to the capital of Mexico, and points south, north, east, and west.

The Thunderbirds proudly accepted the challenge of the sweptwing "F" and found that the higher performance characteristics, including a faster rate of roll, made possible the addition of new maneuvers.

While the Thunderbird team was being formed at Luke Air Force Base in Arizona, a new jet fighter was making its appearance just a few hundred miles away at the Flight Test Center at Edwards Air Force Base, California. This new plane, heavier, longer and higher than the F-84's, was made by the North American Aviation corporation. They called it the F-100 Super Sabre—the first of the "century" series and a plane with a special destiny. The Super Sabre would take man into the supersonic age, for the Super Sabre was the first operational jet to exceed the speed of sound in level flight.

Just three years later, the Thunderbirds would step from the Thunderstreak to the Super Sabre to become the world's first supersonic aerial demonstration team. The F-100 would also provide the team with more flight hours and more air miles than any other aircraft. In it they would fly two oceans and would demonstrate their

The Plane Is Important   81

prowess before millions of people on all five continents. It was in 1953 that Lt. Col. Frank K. "Pete" Everest, the first Air Force officer to fly the new F-100, screamed over the fifteen-kilometer course of California's Salton Sea in scorching low-altitude runs of 767 and 752 miles per hour for an average speed of 755.149 miles per hour and the fastest speed passes ever recorded to that time by the National Aeronautics Association. In August 1955, Col. Horace Hanes bettered the record when he took a "C" model F-100 to a speed of 822.135 miles an hour; later models were clocked at more than 1,000 miles an hour.

These speeds are possible because the Super Sabre has been specially designed for supersonic flight. Its engineers planned it that way.

The wings and tail sweep back to an angle of 45 degrees. A special heat-resistant metal called titanium is used extensively throughout the plane, while a low-drag, ultra-streamlined fuselage and canopy with only one air-intake duct help make supersonic flight possible.

Special flaps in the wings' leading edges slide in and out to change the flow of air across the wing and give the F-100 greater lift and ease of control. This movement is determined by speed and the angle of the wing in flight. At the slower takeoff and landing speeds, for instance, the leading edge slides forward and down.

An additional safety feature, new in the F-100 but now quite common, is the drag chute, which pops out from the rear of the plane to slow it down and shorten the landing roll. The Thunderbirds' drag chutes are, quite naturally, red, white, and blue.

Compared with the F-84F Thunderstreak, the Super Sabre is a monster. The swept-back wings have a span of

The Six-Ship Wedge in the final flat pass before the audience at a Thunderbird demonstration. *Courtesy U.S. Air Force*

38 feet, 9 inches; the ship is 53 feet, 11 inches in length, and stands 15 feet high.

The team, then, was taking off in a plane that was ten feet longer, with a wing span five feet greater, and a foot taller than the F-84F. The Super Sabre was a "bird" born to fight—in air-to-air combat and as a fighter-bomber to provide ground support for our army troops.

The Plane Is Important 83

Now it would also dance through the sky with the Thunderbirds at the controls.

From 1956 until 1964, the Thunderbirds flew their Super Sabres in 641 performances, thrilling 48 million spectators on five continents. In 1960 another jet fighter-bomber, the F-105 Thunderchief, became operational, and in 1964, the team moved into Republic Aviation's Thunderchief. For four months they would lift off the runway in this sleek new aircraft.

The Thunderchief first served in combat in Vietnam, where it fights side by side with the Super Sabre.

It was a standard operational fighter when the Thunderbirds first saw it, but several modifications were made to tailor it more specifically to aerobatic work.

The Doppler radar system was removed to provide space for the Thunderbirds to carry their special apparel in a built-in suitcase.

Because liquid oxygen is unavailable in many countries of the world, the oxygen system was equipped to permit the use of high-pressure as well as liquid oxygen; the communications system was also changed to make it easier for the team to operate in foreign lands. The fuel system was modified to make inverted flight possible for an extended period of time, and the afterburner was set to light immediately instead of with a five-second delay. A show panel was added to the regular instrument panel just for the Thunderbirds.

The F-105's greater power made new maneuvers possible. When the team presented its first official demonstration in the Thunderchiefs at the Azalea Festival in Norfolk, Virginia, on April 26, the audience was treated to the first five- and six-ship formations ever given by the Thunderbirds.

Then, at 6:41 P.M. on May 9, 1964, the Thunderbird

diamond approached the runway at Hamilton Air Force Base, California. They had just presented their sixth show in the Thunderchief at McChord Air Force Base, Washington. The seventh was scheduled for the following day at Hamilton's Armed Forces Day open house. Maj. Paul Kauttu in Thunderbird One made his tactical pitchup for the landing. He would be followed immediately by Capt. Eugene Devlin, left wingman, in Thunderbird Two. As Captain Devlin made his pitchup, something happened. With shocking suddenness, the F-105 disintegrated in the air.

Captain Devlin's tragic death in the wreckage of his Thunderchief canceled the scheduled performance, and, as a result, the team's remaining F-105's were ordered to Mobile Air Matériel Area at Brookley Air Force Base, Alabama, for an immediate and thorough inspection. The Air Force was determined that no other Thunderbird pilot would meet the same fate.

Meanwhile the Air Force scheduled its entire Thunderchief fleet for modification.

Aircraft from combat wings naturally held priority over the Thunderbirds, and the team faced the prospect of a period of several months during which it would be left without aircraft in which to perform.

High-level conferences were called to resolve the dilemma. On June 25, Maj. Ed Palmgren, commander of the Thunderbirds, received a phone call from Gen. Walter C. Sweeney, commander of Tactical Air Command. A decision had been reached: Major Palmgren was to report immediately to TAC Headquarters at Langley Air Force Base, Virginia.

He arrived at Langley at noon the following day. There he was told that the Thunderbirds would return as soon as possible to the Super Sabre—the more powerful F-100D model.

Five days later, six F-100D's were delivered to the team from the 4510th Combat Crew Training Wing at Luke Air Force Base, Arizona. At the same time the six were delivered to the Thunderbirds at Nellis, two others were flown to the North American Aviation Company plant at Palmdale, California, for slight modification and painting with the Thunderbird colors. As two Super Sabres were completed at Palmdale, two others were brought in from the Thunderbirds. By July 20, all eight F-100D's were in place at Nellis. The nine Super Sabres were ready to resume the interrupted show schedule. Although only six aircraft are used in a performance, the team actually has nine assigned. The two spare "D" models make it possible to travel with one on hand—just in case—and still schedule the other aircraft for periodic maintenance work at the home hangar. The two-seat F-100F used for demonstration rides had remained with the team even after the conversion to the F-105.

On August 1, less than three months after the tragedy, the Thunderbirds had returned to the Super Sabre and were back on the road.

9

Inside the Engine

Now let's take a look at the J-57 jet engine inside the Super Sabre to find out just what gives the Thunderbirds that tremendous speed, power, and thrust as they perform their aerial maneuvers.

The Thunderbird maintenance crew are busy men as they go about the important job of keeping the Super Sabres in top condition. Hoping to find a mechanic with some time to spare, I went down to the Thunderbirds' home on the flight line at Nellis Air Force Base.

The shiny aluminum sides glinted under the hot Nevada sun. The huge building stretches for nearly a block along the flight-line apron. Giant doors at one end slide open to admit the Super Sabres. There's space enough on the spotless hangar floor for all nine F-100's, with room to spare. In a locker room just off the hangar area, the Thunderbirds "suit up" in their parachutes, G-suits, and helmets. Here, too, are the offices for the pilots, the main-

Staff Sgt. Clayton H. Adams, Jr. (in T-shirt) at work on the tail section of a J-57 jet engine that has been removed from a Thunderbird plane. *Courtesy U.S. Air Force*

tenance crew, and the administrative force. Whenever the team is home, the whole building echoes with sound; when they're on the road, it is very quiet.

It was bustling with activity this particular day. The team *was* home, and some of the aircraft were undergoing maintenance. I found Staff Sgt. Clayton Adams, Jr., a jet-engine specialist with a great deal of knowledge about the engine and time to answer some questions.

Sergeant Adams led me to a section of the hangar where the Pratt and Whitney J-57 engine (looking like a giant black stovepipe) had just been removed from Maj. Paul Kauttu's Thunderbird One. It rested on its special cart, and we poked around among the vast assortment of wires and tubes. I marveled at the complexity of this power plant that propels the Thunderbirds through the air.

He pointed out the various parts of the engine. In the forward section is the self-starting unit that makes it possible for the Thunderbirds to start engines anywhere in the world without the use of an outside ground power unit to light the fire in the engine. Next, he pointed to the compressor, the number-one turbine, the first basket or burner can, two more compressors, and three main turbine wheels. This brought us back to the tail section. If the engine had been in operation, the hot blast from the exhaust would have made it impossible to approach.

But the fire was out; the engine was cold. Sergeant Adams put his hand on the shiny flaps at the end of the tailpipe.

"These are called eyelids," he explained as he pushed them back and forth. Suddenly he turned and, with a mischievous smile, said, "I'll bet you think a jet is propelled forward by the hot gases pushing against the air in back."

I fell neatly into his trap. "It certainly sounds reasonable."

He grinned with delight at being able to explain the theory of jet propulsion.

"A lot of people make that mistake. The jet plane isn't pushed forward by the gas escaping from the rear; rather it is propelled forward by the reaction of the rearward force." He ran his hand over the long black tailpipe of the engine, his trained eyes automatically checking every inch of it. "If you studied physics in high school, you probably remember Sir Isaac Newton and his third law of motion—that for every action there is an equal and opposite reaction. In the jet the air is collected and accelerated rearward to a high velocity, and the reaction to the force applied in doing that is transmitted to the aircraft in forward thrust."

"It sounds complicated," I said.

"Not at all." He motioned me toward his office. He rummaged through his desk and magically produced a child's balloon. He began to inflate it. His cheeks puffed out and his eyes sparkled at me. When the balloon was a long, plump sausage shape, he pinched the neck closed and held it high over his head. He let go and the balloon swooshed through the air to land in a crumpled, deflated heap at the feet of a master sergeant just coming through the door. He picked it up and dangled it playfully in front of him. "Explaining the jet theory, eh?"

Sergeant Adams retrieved his balloon and stuffed it back into his desk. "Yep." He turned back to me. "When I inflated the balloon, air was forced into it under pressure. When I turned it loose, part of the air escaped through the small opening at the back. This reduced the pressure of the air inside that end of the balloon. The air at the front end, being greater, pushed it forward so that it sailed over our heads."

I thought of the complicated piece of machinery in the hangar. "How do you apply this same idea to the operation of the jet engine?"

"If you can keep the picture of the balloon in mind," he replied, "imagine that you could add fuel and heat the air inside of it. The jet engine is simply a mechanical device that produces the same forward thrust by taking a mass of air, compressing it, combining it with fuel, heating it, and forcing it rearward through an opening."

"That's all? You just add fuel, heat the air, compress it, and whoosh—you get power like the Thunderbirds'?"

"Well, it's not quite *that* simple." He walked to a bookcase and pulled out a thick technical manual for the J-57 engine. Flipping the pages to a cutaway drawing of the engine, he began to explain what happens when a Thunderbird pilot presses the button of his self-starting unit.

"Pushing the starter button energizes the system by drawing power from the battery. Air and fuel are brought together in the starter combustion chamber, where a spark plug has been activated to create a spark igniting the mixture."

His finger traced along the electric and fuel lines. "The mixed air and fuel, when ignited, produce tremendous compression and heat. Superheated gases strike the starter turbine and send it spinning at more than 350,000 revolutions per minute."

We studied the diagram, and he showed me how the turbine feeds power into the gears of a drive-shaft system. This forces a high-speed rotor to pass energy to the compressor in the forward section of the engine.

He went on. "As the compressor spins, it sucks in air through the front intake, and the result is pressure in what is known as the fire basket or burner can. This looks much like the inside of an old-fashioned stovepipe. As pressure builds up, the compressor in the forward section begins to spin and, at the same time, the number-two and number-three compressors spin, too. When the spinning reaches 12 to 16 percent of its maximum revolutions per minute, the pilot lights the fire within the engine itself.

"The pilot pushes his throttle forward to idle, the fuel rushes in and sprays through a nozzle into the burner can. Air swoops in and meets the fuel. Ignited by two spark plugs, the air-fuel mixture begins to burn at a tremendous 4,000 degrees Fahrenheit. It expands, sweeps across the three main turbine wheels, and the result is an acceleration that speeds up the entire engine. The starter unit cuts out and the Super Sabre is alive with its own power."

He snapped the book closed.

"And that takes you from the simple idea of a balloon creating forward thrust by reducing the pressure within it to the more complicated process of starting a jet engine by combining air, fuel, and heat to create the same kind of pressure and thrust when the pilot takes his ship into the air."

"Whew! It certainly must keep you mechanics busy making sure all those engine parts are in perfect working order," I said as we started back toward the hangar.

"Yes, it is a big job," he admitted. "And every man who works on these 'birds' is proud of the tradition that no show has ever been canceled because the aircraft weren't ready to fly."

We watched the crew returning the engine to Thunderbird One.

"How about the extra thrust the Thunderbirds use in some of their maneuvers?"

"You mean the AB or afterburner?"

"Yes. What is it and how does it work?"

Sergeant Adams walked again to the rear of the big engine. The gaping black hole of the exhaust was large enough for a man to crawl into.

"When the pilot pushes his throttle slightly to the left and forward, he kicks in the AB. Remember, I mentioned these eyelids." He pointed again to the special flaps on the tailpipe exhaust. "These move open when the AB is operating. The afterburner is a specially designed section of the exhaust system. More fuel is injected into the engine airstream behind the turbines. This fuel is burned with some of the air not previously used for the main combustion process. This extra addition of heat causes

A last-minute problem with an F-100 Super Sabre brings forth a crew of fast-working maintenance men just before a Thunderbird show at Williams Air Force Base, Arizona. *Courtesy U.S. Air Force*

the stream to be ejected from the jet pipe nozzle at an increased velocity, thus increasing the thrust."

"We've talked a lot about engine thrust, but what is it?" I wanted to clear up all the points about which I was curious.

"Thrust is measured in pounds. It is a force which must be applied through a distance for work to be done. Since horsepower is a measurement of the rate of doing work, we can say that when the Super Sabre is thundering through the air at 850 miles an hour, with its afterburner increasing the thrust from a normal 10,200 pounds to 16,000 pounds, the bird is putting out 37,000 horsepower."

"That's a tremendous amount of power," I agreed. Sergeant Adams was about to return to his work when I remembered one more puzzling item. "But, what makes the smoke?"

He turned back. "I knew I'd forgotten something. The smoke was added to the Thunderbird aircraft to make it easier for the audience to follow the maneuvers through the air. It's quite a simple device, really. We just added a valve and a pump to the aft fuel cell so that it can be cut out of the fuel system and filled with engine oil instead of fuel. A tube leads from the cell and juts out over the tailpipe with its nozzle pointing down into the jet stream. The oil spraying down into the flaming exhaust vaporizes and produces white smoke. The pilot can turn the spray on and off from the cockpit. He has enough oil for about fifteen minutes of smoke during each show."

Having explored the jet engine from intake to tailpipe, I thanked Sergeant Adams for his time and patience. Now that the mechanics of the jet were fresh in my mind, I wanted to talk to a pilot who could explain just what it's like to fly in Thunderbird One as flight leader.

10

Leading the Team

The Thunderbird leader sits behind his desk in the flight leader's office. On the walls around him are framed reminders of other teams, other leaders. Just outside, the long hall is crowded with mementos of Thunderbird history—the keys to cities, photos of former team members, plaques, citations, and other honors.

How does a man feel about taking over the leadership of a team that is already known to millions of people all over the world? Is there a sense of competition—a doubt, perhaps, that his team won't quite shape up to those that have gone before?

I talked to several of the Thunderbird leaders. Here are some of the thoughts they have about being in that number-one slot.

"A leader can never compete with a former leader. Each in his own way is unique and makes the team an extension of himself. He helps the team grow and expand

and become better; not because the pilots are better than the former team, but because it is a natural evolution. They are bound to be better now than they were five or ten years ago. When someone tells me it's the best Thunderbird show they've ever seen, I don't take it as a personal tribute to my leadership. It's more an indication that the team is growing in stature. A leader can't let the team be stereotyped. It must keep going, and about the only way to do it is with new maneuvers or new twists to old maneuvers."

Maj. Paul Kauttu is the only Thunderbird ever to step from a position on the team to the job of flight leader. He flew slot in 1963, was promoted to major in 1964, and asked if he would take the leader's position. He said yes and extended his Thunderbird tour for an additional two years. In 1967 he was promoted to lieutenant colonel.

One of the first things he discovered as leader was the great difference in flying as Thunderbird One and as the man in the slot. As I talked with him, he leaned back in his chair, studied a photo of the four-ship diamond on the wall in front of him, and said, "The team seldom spends more than a minute or a minute and a half in any formation before they switch to another. This is where the slot man and wingmen have to work.

"When I became leader, I entered an entirely different environment. The physical part was left behind. I discovered that the other positions were plain hard work where you must pay strict attention to what's going on. Our other team members landed after a show with their flight suits soaked in sweat. As leader I found that I was landing with my flight suit bone-dry." He smiled and his face took on a boyish enthusiasm that belied his maturity.

Being the leader is not the easiest job in the world, and he realized he had made it sound almost too simple.

"This doesn't mean that I don't have a lot to think about up there. I do. My responsibility is for the timing and the distance from the ground when we bottom out on maneuvers. A good show depends a lot on timing. If the team flies a sloppy show, it's the leader who gets the blame."

But the Thunderbirds, as any audience will tell you, seldom fly a sloppy show. What is it like to experience a Thunderbird demonstration from the position of leader? Here in his own words is the story of one leader of a Thunderbird show from beginning to end.

"The leader first makes a survey flight of every show site to check the demonstration area. He flies in a light aircraft and checks the terrain for any unusual features which must be watched for during the show. Some of the things he looks for are trees, poles, radar antennas, buildings. He can then alert the pilots, especially the solos who fly lower than the others.

"He also meets with Federal Aviation Agency officials to determine any altitude or flight restrictions. Perhaps there is a hospital over which they must not fly, or there may be certain altitude restrictions in the area. The FAA issues directives to all other aircraft, especially private light planes, to clear the area for an altitude of fifteen thousand feet and a radius of five miles of the show site.

"An hour and a half before takeoff there is a detailed briefing with myself, the five pilots, and the narrator. Any information I have is given at this time, and the narrator is told of anything that might make it necessary to change the wording of his script.

"Twenty minutes before show time, the crew chiefs carefully check the aircraft. Seven minutes before takeoff the pilots gather in front of their aircraft; they climb the ladders together, make cockpit checks. At one minute before takeoff I give the signal to start engines. The flight chief snaps a hand salute. As his hand drops, we hit the starter buttons in unison and turn our radios to the special Thunderbird frequency. This is a radio frequency that no other aircraft in the area is using, so that it will always be clear for my signals and those of any other pilot calling changes in formation.

"I say, 'Okay, Thunderbirds, we're taking off on runway zero-two to the north, altimeter two-nine-nine-two; EPR (exhaust pressure ratio) two-point-zero-six; check your lanyards.'

"Each pilot then checks in with me. 'Two-three-four-five-six.'

"The aircraft are made ready for taxi and I say, 'Speed breaks up, ready, now!' Then, 'Flaps down, ready, now!' There is a pause while the flaps travel all the way down, then I say, 'Flaps intermediate, ready, now!' and the flaps are brought back halfway.

"We are ready for takeoff, but before we begin our roll, the crew chiefs make a final visual check of the aircraft, and we pilots make a final flight-control check to determine that all flight controls are working properly.

"I say, 'Stand by canopies, canopies part closed, ready, now.'

"The team lowers the canopies partway in unison. When the canopies are all at the same height, I say, 'Hand salute, ready, now.' Each pilot salutes his crew chief and is saluted in return. We are now ready to start our taxi.

"I say, 'Let's push 'em up, it'll be a left turn.'

"The aircraft taxi down the apron, nose to tail with about one to one and a half feet separation until they

Breaking ground together, the Thunderbirds lift their Super Sabres into the air. *Courtesy U.S. Air Force*

reach the end of the runway. I then receive my takeoff clearance from the control tower and the diamond lines up in fingertip formation, with the slot on the right wing of number three or the right wingman. There is yet another check to make sure that all cockpit warning lights are out.

"I say, 'Lead lights out.'

"We are now ready to go when each Thunderbird checks in: 'Two lights out, Three lights out,' and so on. Then I say, 'Okay, Thunderbirds, let's run 'em up.'

"We push our throttles to full military thrust and make one last check. I look at Number Two, who gives me a signal—a nod, a wave of the hand, or a salute. I then look at Number Three, who gives me a signal and,

Leading the Team 99

The six Thunderbird demonstration pilots join together in wedge formation bottoming out of a Six-Ship Loop. *Courtesy U.S. Air Force*

in turn, has received a similar signal from Number Four.

"Then I say, 'Thunderbirds release brakes, ready, now.' I follow this immediately by: 'AB's on, ready, now!'

"We roll down the runway together. At 150 knots, I call 'Nose gear,' and the four aircraft raise their nose wheels; the slot calls, 'Four in,' and the diamond is complete.

"I pull into a 60-degree climb so the audience can get a good view of the diamond as it makes its maximum performance climb.

"We then turn out for the opening maneuver—the Diamond Cloverleaf.

"I watch the show site and position the formation. About three miles out, we turn and come directly in toward the audience, rolling the diamond. I call, 'Thunderbirds rolling in for a high show.' The Diamond Cloverleaf is next.

"Fifty feet above the ground and at 400 knots airspeed I say, 'Stand by smoke, smoke on, ready, now!' As the formation approaches, I announce, 'Nose coming up.' Then, at vertical, I call, 'Rolling left and rolling.' We go over the top at 6,500 feet and 125 knots."

For the next thirty minutes the leader will make the performance as smooth as possible so that the wingmen don't have to work so hard to keep in formation with him. He will also try to make the show as nearly perfect as possible for the delight of the audience watching below.

He starts to think of the next maneuver while completing the one in progress. Besides positioning the aircraft, he must also think of the timing between the diamond and the solos. He must make last-minute adjustments in the formation to keep the show running smoothly.

He keeps up a constant chatter with the other pilots by radio about the timing for the maneuver, etc. He has to think about the wind in order to make sure that the formation hits the show center on time. He knows what the wind is when he takes off, but it can change both in velocity and direction at any time during the show. During the first few maneuvers he must establish what the wind velocity is and its direction for proper positioning.

As the leader he must also always strive for the exact airspeed without which the maneuvers would be impossible. The positioning of the formation to have the right airspeed at the right time is constantly on his mind.

The leader must also remember that there is a possibility of an emergency. What action will he take if one aircraft aborts? Sometimes the pilot can land, hop into the spare, and rejoin the formation, but there isn't always time. If the leader aborts, the show will be canceled. If any other man fails to take off or must turn back, it is possible to continue, but it is the leader who must make the decision and who must be ready to make it immediately.

There is far more to being Thunderbird One than simply donning a beautiful white show suit and going up in a F-100 Super Sabre for thirty minutes of "fun flying." It is this kind of responsibility that makes each of the Thunderbirds' leaders a very special person, a man who possesses a particular brand of courage that makes him outstanding not only as a fighter pilot but as a leader of men.

Through the end of 1967, the Thunderbirds had only nine flight leaders, and all had unusual records before coming to the Thunderbirds:

Lt. Col. Dick Catledge was an outstanding athlete and received several medals and presidential citations for his World War Two flying before he was shot down behind enemy lines. He became the first Thunderbird leader in 1953.

Capt. Jacksel M. Broughton played left tackle for West Point from 1942 to 1944; completed his West Point studies in three years; flew 114 missions in Korea. The Distinguished Flying Cross is among his many combat medals.

Maj. J. A. Robinson—"Robbie"—took the first F-86 Sabrejets into combat in Korea with the Fourth Fighter Group and flew 74 missions.

Maj. Robert S. Fitzgerald, one of the most colorful leaders, flew over 340 hours of combat time as a B-24 bomber pilot in World War Two and was a member of the Fenton and Fitzgerald aerobatic team in 1947 and 1948.

Later, he became an airline pilot with Pan American World Airways. During the Korean conflict he flew twenty missions in the F-84, and in 1953 became right wingman with the Air Force's aerobatic team in Europe, The Skyblazers. He was the first Thunderbird leader to be killed. He died in a crash in 1961 while on a training mission with the Thunderbirds. Fitzgerald Boulevard, the main street at Nellis Air Force Base, is named in his honor.

Maj. Ralph D. "Hoot" Gibson was one of America's first jet aces. He served in Korea, flying the F-86 Sabre jet. He was awarded the Silver Star twice for gallantry while leading his F-86s against overwhelming odds.

Maj. Ed. "Lucky" Palmgren became the first team member to serve a second tour when he returned as leader in 1963. From 1954 to 1956 he flew solo and slot. A veteran of World War Two, he took part in four invasions as a signalman aboard an LST with the U.S. Navy. In 1954 he gave up his place in the Bendix Trophy Race to help a fellow pilot in distress.

Maj. Paul Kauttu tried three times to join the Thunderbirds before he was successful. He is the first man to go from a position on the team to leader. He is a Korean veteran. In 1955, while serving a tour in the Far East, he was leader of an aerobatic team on Okinawa.

Lt. Col. Ralph Maglione flew 104 Korean combat missions and holds the Silver Star, the Distinguished Flying Cross, the Air Medal with five Oakleaf Clusters, and the Purple Heart. Prior to joining the Thunderbirds he served on the air staff at the Pentagon, where he completed study for a Bachelor of Arts degree at the University of Maryland.

In July, 1967, Maj. Neil L. Eddins became the second pilot to return for another Thunderbird tour when he took over as the ninth leader of the team. Major Eddins is the first veteran of the war in Vietnam to lead the men of the Thunderbirds. In June 1966 he went to Southeast Asia, where he logged 106 combat missions in the F-105 Thunderchief—100 of these were flown over North Vietnam. From April 1959 until April 1961, he flew the slot position with the team.

11

Flying on the Wings

Along with leadership and practice, there is another fac-
tor of vital importance in formation aerobatics—faith in
the wingman. It has been said that a good wingman is
like "a second pair of eyes," and one Thunderbird leader
has said that he thinks the wingmen work the hardest in
any Thunderbird show.

In order to put a formation through rolls and turns as
though the four ships were a single unit, the wingmen
must continually play the throttle and follow the movement of the leader's wing tips—maintaining constant position beneath them. "We're working and pulling the
stick against nose-down trim like mad the whole time,"
a wingman will tell you. "I work under a constant four-
to-five-g pull throughout the show."

With this in mind I wanted to talk to the Thunderbirds' right and left wingmen and see what it was like to
fly a show on the wings with the diamond formation.

This is the maze of gauges, switches, and dials that every Thunderbird pilot faces when he climbs into the cockpit of his F-100 Super Sabre. He must keep an eye on all of them while flying close formation at near-supersonic speed. *Courtesy North American Aviation, Inc.*

I found the Thunderbirds' right wingman down in the hangar checking his aircraft. Together we squeezed atop the ladder and looked into the cockpit to see exactly what he had to work with. The pilot uses the throttle, stick, and rudder pedals to control the aircraft in the precision aerobatics. The controls of the Super Sabre aren't at all what one would expect in an airplane that skims through the air with such deft precision and control. The right wingman pointed to a thick tube with ridges running around it on the left of the cockpit. "This is the throttle," he said. "When I move it forward, it increases power, when I move it back it eases off on all that horsepower in the big J-57 engine. It also controls the afterburner. When I push the throttle all the way forward in maximum power position, the engine is blowing out a static thrust of 10,200 pounds. When I push the throttle slightly to the left and forward again, the afterburner kicks in. Suddenly that thrust is up to 16,000 pounds. Instead of being just a plain, ordinary throttle, this control also has several subcontrols. On top is the speed-brake switch. When I push the switch back, a big speed brake rams out into the airstream from the belly of the aircraft. In a second the smooth flight turns into a rumbling roar and the plane slows rapidly. I retract the brake by pushing the switch forward.

"On the side of the throttle is a microphone switch. When I press in with my thumb, I position the radio for calls to other aircraft or to ground stations. And then there is this small button on the side of the throttle for smoke control."

He then showed me the control stick. It had a molded grip curved to fit a pilot's hand. It was like holding the grip of a target pistol that had been fashioned with extreme care to provide the maximum comfort and use of the fingers. It is a complete control system in itself. "Years ago," he told me, "this used to be called a joy stick. I suppose the name came from a barnstorming pilot who found happiness only when flying high in the sky."

He continued to tell me something about the stick and its uses. "In addition to operating the basic controls of flight—the ailerons and the tail—the grip also contains the trim switch, which faces me. By thumbing this switch to the left or right I trim the airplane for lateral or rolling flight; by moving the switch forward and backward I control the pitch or up-and-down trim. But," he said, "you wanted to know what it's like to fly on the wings in a Thunderbird demonstration. Let's go upstairs and I'll see if I can describe a Thunderbird show from the point of view of the wingman." We climbed down from the ladder and went in to settle in the Thunderbird conference room, where he began his description of a typical Thunderbird show from his viewpoint.

"Much of what I tell you," he said, "will apply equally to the left wing." The left wingman had joined us, and he nodded his head in agreement.

The right wingman went on with his description of flying on the wings in a Thunderbird demonstration.

"We approach the takeoff runway in doubled-up formation with the left wing on the leader's wing, the slot taxiing on my right wing. I move into position on the leader's right. We lower our canopies and run up the engines. As they are running up, we slip into nose-down trim. I check to see if the slot is ready. He gives me a salute and I give the leader a windup signal.

"We release brakes and start the afterburners. At lift-off I stay a little high, to avoid choppiness, and snap the gear up immediately because the slot man will go under my aircraft to slip into his position. As soon as the slot is in, I drop a little until I'm flying low on the leader's wing

---

The two wingmen have slipped back over the slot to fly the Arrowhead Loop—one of their most famous formations. *Courtesy U.S. Air Force*

—in AB position to balance on the slot. We then swing into the Diamond Cloverleaf opener. As the diamond exits from their first maneuver, I trim off the back pressure a little to relax my arm.

"On the next diamond roll I use full nose-down trim for a flat roll with lots of rudder and pullback for the Arrowhead."

"That is one of the newer formations, isn't it?" I asked.

"Yes. It's only been in the show for a few years." He went on to describe this particularly difficult formation.

"When the left wingman says, 'Arrowhead,' and gives the signal, 'Now,' he and I move back far over the slot man's wings, maintaining the three-foot overlap all the while; then we drop back down to fly on the slot for the Arrowhead formation. As we approach the vertical in the Arrowhead loop, I call out over my radio, 'Let's cheat.' This is the signal to move forward three feet. We won't have power for this at the top of the loop; then we coast back down to keep our position. The leader lets up the pressure on the backside of the loop and we exit in a Whifferdill.

"Then I say 'Diamond,' and give the signal to reverse the process and come back over the slot's wings and into our normal diamond position. While in the Whifferdill, the leader announces the next maneuver: 'Changeover Roll next.'

"When we have about 90 degrees of the turn left to go, the slot calls, 'Trail, ready, now.' The diamond then forms into the Trail position. To achieve this, I drop back behind the leader, staying low to keep the tail down and out of the jet wash from the leader's plane. At 90 degrees of roll I call, 'Thunderbirds change, ready, now.' We then change back to the diamond.

"You never look at the ground or the surrounding sky —you keep your eyes on the leader and do every maneuver on the lead plane. We try to make the Changeover in the roll at 270 degrees. And at 360 degrees we exit the show area.

"The next is the Trail Roll, which is the 360-degree roll done in trail formation, with the aircraft flying one behind the other and slightly low to escape the hot backwash from the tail pipe of the plane in front. We exit right and I call, 'Diamond ready, now,' and the diamond reforms.

"I call most of the signals. This is because the others can see to follow me if my radio happens to go out. For this reason my aircraft usually makes the first move.

"In the Five-Card Loop, for instance, I will say 'Thunderbirds, Card,' and on the signal, 'Now,' I move up to fly line abreast of the leader, while the left wing moves back and the slot stays in the center to form the five spot. The solo comes in to fly line abreast with the left wingman.

"All the pilots have gimmicks to help keep the proper alignment. In this one, for instance, I may use the canopy bow of the leader's plane to line up laterally and the lights on the wing tips to line up the fuselages so that they're even.

"When I say, 'Diamond,' and give the signal, the solo breaks off and the diamond moves back into position.

"In the Bonton Roulle, the left wingman calls the signal, 'Let's go.' He may even say it in Spanish, '*Arriba*' or whatever he and I have developed between us. However, we never change the signals, so that the other pilots are not confused. We're coming by for the Bonton Roulle and the team is sure of that, because signals are always the same no matter what form they may take.

"As the leader starts his nose up, he calls, 'Go explosion,' and we move out and each roll in place. This is one maneuver when we work independently without being relative to the leader. We use our afterburners to get back into the diamond formation and prepare for the Line Abreast Loop.

"As we pull up and reach the vertical, the signal, 'Thunderbirds, Line Abreast, ready, now,' I and the left wingman move up to fly line abreast with the leader. I must be sure to leave room for the slot to slip in between me and the leader. We all bottom out and exit—still line abreast.

"The diamond reforms and we come back for the Arrowhead Roll done at a 90-degree angle to the show line. At the signal, 'Thunderbirds, Arrowhead,' and then, 'Now,' we again slip over the slot's wing into the Arrowhead formation, go up, and roll.

"Then comes the Changeover Cloverleaf, which begins 90 degrees before we get to the show center, when the slot calls, 'Let's go Trail,' and the familiar, 'Ready, now.' We enter the show area in trail formation and begin our climb. Just before reaching the vertical, I say, 'Thunderbirds, change, ready, now.' The change is made back to the diamond, with the leader doing a 90-degree roll and a complete loop; the diamond ends up perpendicular to the show line and exits.

"Away from the show line and spectators, the diamond's Whifferdill turns us around quickly and brings us back facing the spectators flying directly toward the crowd, for the Bomb Burst. We pull up into the vertical and the leader calls, 'Stand by, break,' and as we reach

The Six-Ship Wedge coming down the back side of a loop to close the show with a Flat Pass and Victory Roll. *Courtesy U.S. Air Force* the vertical, he adds, 'Break, ready, now.' I pull 90 degrees to the right and pull on through six- or seven-thousand feet altitude. I fly straight out for about two miles. When I hear the leader say, 'Stand by, split-S, split-S, ready, now,' I roll 180 degrees and dive straight down. This is the first time in the show that I have had a chance to see the ground.

"I set the altitude and the left wing matches it. We approach the flat area at 480 knots, thirty feet above the ground. Just as we approach the crossover, the leader calls for AB's, and as we hit the crossover, we turn our smoke off. I roll 360 degrees, go straight up and loop.

"Coming down the back side of the loop, I meet the leader; the left wing and slot come in and the solos join us for the Six-Ship Roll, Whifferdill, and Six-Ship Loop. During this final loop, I can finally take my right hand off the stick for a rest and fly with my left. I even have a chance to wave a cheery greeting to the slot man. There is one final U-turn for the flat pass inside the show line. Then we turn on our afterburners to come in for a simultaneous "blam" finish. As we pull up and around, we line up the crossing point. Thunderbird Four says, 'Let's go T, ready, now.' We move into Trail formation while the solos come in to fly line abreast of the leader. As we make a vertical approach, I call, 'Change, ready, now,' and the Diamond forms. The solos shoot off to the side while we roar in, roll 90 degrees, do a complete loop, and come out right down the show line to bottom out. The show's over, and we prepare for our spectacular landing.

"The leader calls, 'Stand by for left pitch,' and each pilot acknowledges the signal received. Then the leader calls, 'Pitching left,' and he enters the traffic pattern followed by the other three in trail formation and in landing pattern. The solos come in for their approach, the lead solo rolls inverted, forming the Calypso Pass down the runway. Finally he snaps over, the two solos pitch up and join the Diamond in the landing pattern."

As someone brought a stack of photos in for the right and left wingmen to autograph, I rose to leave. There was one more position I wanted to investigate. I had to talk to the final man in the diamond formation—the man in the slot.

12

The Man in the Slot

Anticipating the leader's every move is the real secret of tight-formation aerobatics, and the Thunderbirds are crackerjacks at it. The wingmen may work the hardest on the turns and maneuvers, but the man who flies the most dangerous position is the man in the slot. He brings up the rear of the Diamond formation, trailing the leader closer at 500 miles per hour than any sane auto driver would tail another car at 20 miles per hour on the highway. It was previously the practice for the slot man to have the leading edge of his plane's tail fin washed down after each show to remove the carbon from the lead plane's exhaust. Now, however, the leading edge is left blackened with carbon as a sort of status symbol for this man who tucks his plane up into the middle of the diamond and flies the show completely surrounded by other aircraft.

All this takes precision timing and coordination of the

highest caliber. We asked the slot man if he would take us into the cockpit and fly a Thunderbird show looking up the tail pipe of the leader's jet plane. He said he couldn't do it in reality, of course. But here in imagination we climb into the slot man's position, tuck ourselves up under the lead plane, and fly a Thunderbird performance. Let's go down to the flight line now as the show opens and the Diamond and solos taxi out for takeoff. Here in his own words is the slot man's view of a Thunderbird show.

"Let's begin right from the beginning," he said.

"I understand," I replied "that you make the first move as the Diamond formation takes off."

"That's right. I must get under the right wingman and get into position as quickly as possible.

"As the diamond and solos taxi out, the leader turns the flight. I take the outside right wing. The first thing I do is lower my seat all the way to the bottom, which gives me a clearer view from the windscreen without having to hunch down to see the leader's aircraft under the canopy bow. This is a bow-shaped piece which is part of the canopy but it is metal and not Plexiglas.

"About this time I begin to get what I call pregame butterflies. This is not caused by fear but by desire to do the best I can.

"The canopies are lowered and the leader gives the signal to start engines. All the team members are excited, I guess, but I'm a little more excited than the others because I'm the one who makes the first move on takeoff. As soon as I feel that I can get my aircraft under the right wing with minimum clearance, I dip the left wing and go directly under the right wingman's aircraft, making straight for the leader. If the right wing didn't pull his landing gear up immediately, I would hit it. However,

The Man in the Slot   117

This dramatic "View from the Slot" was painted for the U.S. Air Force by artist Keith Ferris. It shows the glowing tail pipe of the leader's plane as seen by the slot pilot just above his canopy bow. The reflection of the pilot's helmet can be seen in the rear-view mirror at the top of the bow. *Courtesy U.S. Air Force*

there is always a place to go in case something goes wrong and I make my move keeping this in mind.

"I'm so low when I make that move, the left wing is dipped until it is only eight to ten inches off the runway. The airflow from the slot plane actually raises the right wingman's airplane slightly. I snap my gear up immediately as I start my move under the right wing.

"As soon as I am in the AB position (the tip of the stabilizer just below the flame pattern of the leader's afterburner) I call, 'Four is in.' I am now looking out the canopy at the leader's plane. As soon as he gets the signal, the leader starts the nose of the formation up. We climb

The famous Thunderbird diamond starts to break from its usual tight formation in preparation for the Bonton Roulle. When each has reached the proper distance, the aircraft will roll in place. *Courtesy U.S. Air Force*

steeply in Diamond formation at about 150 knots and at the top of the climb make the turn for the first maneuver—the Cloverleaf.

"Once the AB's are off, I move into my normal slot position, which is with the tail and top of the canopy in the jet wash of the leader's plane and the pitot tube or airspeed indicator under the leader's tail pipe.

"Each time the afterburners are cut in, I must drop a few feet to get the tail and canopy out of the AB flame of the leader's plane, which pushes the jet-blast temperature from a normal 1,100 degrees Fahrenheit to 2,900 degrees Fahrenheit. There is a stainless-steel strip around the leading edge of my stabilizer to absorb the initial blast from the AB. My plane shakes constantly from the airflow of the leader's plane. The crew chief checks it especially carefully after each show for loose or lost screws and rivets.

"The whole show requires a tremendous amount of work, and I come down with my flight suit soaked with perspiration.

"To make the aircraft less sensitive, I fly with a nose-down trim, keeping a 25- to 45-pound pressure all during the show. As we come in for the opening maneuver, the Diamond Cloverleaf, everybody is excited and edgy. It's like the first contact with the opponent in a football game. If there is a good bottom-out of the first maneuver, everyone gets the feeling that we're off to a good start.

"In the diamond formation, the leader shoots for $3\frac{1}{2}$ g's on the pull-up. We come in for the Bonton Roulle, in which the whole Diamond spreads out, and as the leader calls, 'Roll, ready, now,' the leader and right wing roll to the right and the left wing and I roll to the left. All I can see at this point are airplanes and wing tips flashing by very rapidly.

"One of the most difficult maneuvers from my point of view is the Arrowhead, where the two wingmen move back over my wings and fly formation on me. This is particularly difficult because of the length of the formation. I must try and fly as smoothly as possible. If I move a little, the wingmen move a little more—spoiling the symmetry of the entire maneuver. There's a great deal of pressure on me to fly evenly during the entire show in spite of any turbulence in the air.

"In the in-trail or follow-the-leader formation, everyone moves forward and down. It is difficult to make this formation look good and it's particularly hard for the leader to fly because he must keep his plane as stable as

The Thunderbirds are a picture of perfect symmetry as they begin to slip effortlessly into the in-trail formation. *Courtesy U.S. Air Force*

possible. If the leader moves, those behind him move a little more, and by the time it gets back to me at the end of the trail, we'd really be wobbling all over the sky. For the In-Trail, I use cross-controlling to move to the right while maintaining alignment. I use full right rudder and left stick—a little like patting your head and rubbing your stomach at the same time.

"One problem here is to roll without getting a snake effect. If you get the snake effect, the planes get out of alignment, and once again the symmetry of the formation is spoiled. When the leader rolls to the left, by the time he's made a 90-degree roll, I have rolled much farther, and it's my job to make this roll while keeping the alignment of the formation.

"Then in the Five-Card Loop, I move to the middle,

where I'm completely boxed in with aircraft. The right wing moves up to fly line abreast with the leader and the second solo comes in to finish the formation."

He added, "No show is ever routine—each is a challenge.

"In the Bomb Burst I make a 180-degree roll while flying straight up. In this maneuver I use 'seat-of-the-pants' flying, for I have no point of reference. I can watch the leader part of the way; the rest of the way is strictly by feel. In the Crossover, I am the man who comes from behind the spectators (1,500 feet to the right) to shoot for a ten-foot separation from the leader's aircraft, matching his altitude. A perfect Crossover puts four aircraft stacked within forty feet of the ground. We are so close that the pilots can hear the pop of the shock wave in the cockpit as the planes cross.

"I match the leader, making all the necessary adjustments in speed, altitude, direction. In this way, only one aircraft is making a movement and we avoid the possibility of a collision, which would be more likely if both aircraft were making corrections at the same time. We are closing in at the rate of 1,350 feet per second, and an aircraft that is half a second off in timing can be 700 feet behind in the crossover.

"As I finish the cross, I pull up into a 7-g climb and come in above the leader, turn upside down and dive straight down in a loop that brings me back behind him in the slot. Meanwhile, the leader has pulled up and executed a Half Cuban Eight. Then we all move in on the leader for a Six-Ship Loop and Roll.

"On the landing, the Diamond comes in right on the deck. The leader pitches straight up 30 degrees, banks left or right. I drop, for when the leader pitches up, it changes the airflow and dips the nose down. I'm once again the closest man to the ground."

I interrupted for a moment, "What do you think is the hardest maneuver for your position?" I asked. He thought for a moment and then said, "I guess it would be the Changeover Roll. The right wingman calls the signal, and when he says, 'Now,' I must light my afterburner and go charging up to keep in place and make it quick. This means that I build up a real 'head of steam,' and now I have the problem of stopping. I go from maximum power at the start of the change to maximum deceleration in the Changeover. I pull the power back hard and lower my speed brakes to slow my aircraft."

The slot men, like the solos, have their adventures in the air, too. One of these happened July 25, 1956, to Ed "Lucky" Palmgren when he was flying the slot as a member of the precision flying team at a show at Maxwell Air Force Base, Alabama. It was a practice session just before the performance for the squadron officers' school graduation exercises. The engine of Lucky's jet failed.

The failure occurred over the city, and Palmgren radioed the Maxwell tower about his trouble. He refused to bail out over the thickly populated area and headed his aircraft instead for an open area southwest of the field.

The plane first touched down in a pasture about three miles from the base, but was traveling at 150 miles an hour at the time and unable to stop. Bouncing and rolling more than 300 yards, the plane plowed through a Western of Alabama rail line, bounced onto Foshee Road, cut down a telephone and a power pole—one with each wing —narrowly missed a house, and skidded another 200 yards before grinding to a halt. All electricity and power service in the area was immediately disrupted. The wings of the plane were badly damaged in striking the poles, and the landing gear was ruined. But Lucky Palmgren walked away, got into the spare aircraft, and flew the show at Maxwell Air Force Base as if nothing had happened. The slot man finished telling me this story of Lucky Palmgren and then rose to leave. "I hope I've given you some idea of what it's like to fly with us."

I got up too, and said, "It certainly sounds as if you have a very special reason for wanting to fly with the Thunderbirds."

"Yes," he said. "We on the team call it 'the burning desire.' If you don't have it, you probably will never even apply for the team."

I went upstairs again to the Thunderbird leader's office to find out just what was meant by the burning desire.

13

The Burning Desire

When a man is a member of the armed forces, it is a nor-
mal thing to be assigned or reassigned to a unit. One day
he receives a set of orders and shortly thereafter he is off
to serve a tour of duty somewhere. But no one is ever
assigned to the Thunderbirds.

Every man must first volunteer to serve with this famous team; then he must be selected from a long list of
applicants all of whom are anxiously awaiting the day
when they will perhaps be chosen. Each has what the
Thunderbirds themselves describe as the burning desire.

Maj. Paul Kauttu became interested in the Thunderbirds the first time he saw the team perform over
McCarran Airport in Las Vegas, Nevada, in 1954. But it
was not until six years later that he applied for the Thunderbirds. Someone else was chosen. Undaunted, he tried
again early in 1962; again he was disappointed. Later in
1962, on the third try, he made the team.

Six members of the Thunderbirds maintenance team use hands and even feet to attach a tail hook to an F-100 Super Sabre. The tail hook can catch the barrier at the end of a runway in case a pilot overshoots his landing. *Courtesy U.S. Air Force*

What makes a man want to be a Thunderbird?

Maj. Kauttu answered the question this way. "Two things. The desire to serve with the best outfit in the Air Force, and the personal satisfaction that comes from knowing you can do the job—one of the top ones in your profession."

Each of the six men in that precision team arcing through the air has eight men on the ground to give him the support he needs.

The men behind the Air Force's precision flying team, the maintenance men of the Thunderbirds, have one thing in common. Though their background and specialties vary, each feels honored to be a part of this select organization, and rightfully so.

Since only a handful of highly skilled men are selected for this unique duty, the competition is stiff. Each of these men is an expert in his area and is a volunteer, often chosen over a hundred other applicants vying for a single vacancy.

Thunderbird airmen won't hesitate to tell you their two years with the team are the most rewarding experience in their careers. In the words of the maintenance supervisor, "Running a maintenance operation with this group of experts is a real pleasure. Seldom does a supervisor find himself with a highly specialized team where every man wants to do the job and knows how."

Many long days, and frequently nights, are spent keeping the Air Force's showcase flyers airborne. Indeed, the superior maintenance record suggests the habit was formed more than a decade ago. A show has never been canceled because of maintenance difficulties since the team was formed in May 1953.

Because of this demand for extra effort, a day off during the show season is rare, but it could happen—anywhere—in Paris, Luxembourg, London, New Orleans, New York, San Francisco, or San Juan. Visiting interesting places ranks high on the fringe-benefit list.

Admittedly, there are many tests of adaptability. "Living out of a suitcase three fourths of the year is no picnic," says a crew chief. Working hours hardly conform to usual standards. In addition, there's no extra pay—not even flight pay, although the Thunderbird support personnel are aloft more than the average professional aircrew man. But these inconveniencies are seldom topics of team conversation. More important are faster and safer methods of changing pumps and troubleshooting electrical systems.

An obvious indication of what the enlisted men feel toward their "birds" is witnessed during every demonstration. They're out there in front of the crowd, eyes fixed on every movement of the jets with the intense interest of avid aviation enthusiasts.

Thunderbirds become closer to each other than brothers. They live, eat, play, travel, and fly together for more than two hundred days a year.

Every pilot is selected for his outstanding flying ability. Most have seen combat. And every man from the squadron commander to the lowest-ranking airman is especially chosen for the qualities that further the team's reputation as America's Ambassadors in Blue. A Thunderbird, whether a pilot, member of the ground crew, or staff, must be an expert in public relations as well as in his particular job. A crowd or a group may see the Thunderbirds only once, but for the audience the entire United States Air Force is symbolized by these men.

A Thunderbird, no matter what his rank or job, must have an outstanding military record. He must be of the highest moral caliber and be recommended by his squadron commander. Even his wife plays a part in the possible selection. She must write a brief letter telling how she feels about her husband's becoming a Thunderbird—and also how she feels about being left alone for so many days of the year.

When a place on the team opens, the records of all the candidates are carefully screened. If it's a case of selecting a new pilot, the original list of some one hundred volunteers is reduced to about ten. These are called to Nellis.

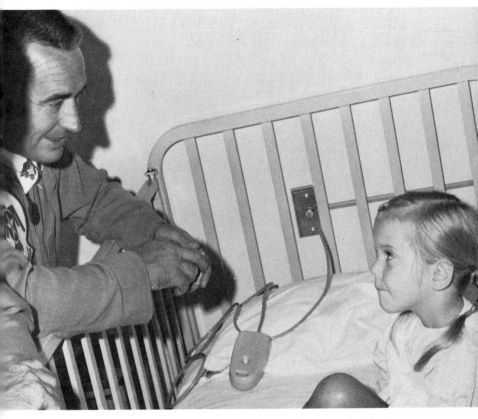

For a Thunderbird pilot it is important to know how to make friends as well as how to fly a jet. *Courtesy U.S. Air Force*

There are searching interviews. The new man flies with the commander in a grueling test of his ability to fly close formation. He feels like the proverbial bug under a microscope. Then the team members sit down together and choose each new member. When you are trying to select the *very best* from a field crowded with *the best,* you can't be too careful. As the list becomes shorter, the tension among the nominees mounts.

The Burning Desire   129

Capt. Ron Catton, a former solo pilot with the team, tells the story of his and Maj. Paul Kauttu's selection for the team:

"Paul and I were attending the University of Omaha on 'Operation Bootstrap.' Paul was at that time stationed at Wright-Patterson Air Force Base, Ohio, and I was stationed at Nellis Air Force Base. We became close friends at Omaha due to our common interest in the Thunderbird aerobatic team and the fact that we were both applicants.

"As time went by and we were notified that we had made each cut, that is to say, we had made the final twenty-five, and then found out that we had made the final ten, and then the final five, our involvement in this thing became stronger and stronger. Our conversation whenever we were together revolved around the Thunderbirds and how we hoped that both of us would make the team.

"If one didn't make it, we wanted the other to make it. We had no idea at this time that the Thunderbirds had any intention of selecting more than one pilot, and so, in this case, whoever was selected would be one of a hundred, so to speak.

"One evening I was studying for an examination. It was mid-April 1962. It was about ten thirty and my telephone rang. I answered the phone and a woman's voice on the other end said, 'Is this Captain Ron Catton?' I said, 'Yes, it is.' She said, 'Congratulations, you have just won yourself a two-year tour with the United States Air Force Thunderbirds!'

"I was spellbound; I couldn't say a word; I was completely dumbfounded. About two minutes later, when I had regained my voice, I found out I was talking with Lynette Brooks, the wife of Capt. Ralph Brooks, who at that time was flying right wing of the Thunderbirds.

Then Ralph came on the line and told me that Paul had also been selected for the team. He asked me to notify him that he had been named to fly the slot position that would be open in September. Paul didn't have a telephone in Omaha.

"I was unable to get hold of Paul that evening, so the next morning I found him in the cafeteria of the student union and asked him to come out in the hall. He did. When we got out in the hall, I said, 'I would like to shake the hand of the new slot pilot of the USAF Thunderbirds.'

"With this, Paul grabbed me by the front of my shirt and almost lifted me off the floor and said that this wasn't something that anyone should kid about and he was very disappointed in me for pulling a trick like this. He went on and on and there I was half hung up. I finally got through to him that I was not kidding, that I had received a call the night before from the Thunderbirds asking me to tell him he had been selected as the new slot man.

"Of course he was very happy there for a few seconds. Then all of a sudden his whole face clouded up and his eyes kind of misted a little bit and he started consoling me for not having made the team (or so he thought). At that time I stuck out my hand and asked him if he wasn't going to shake hands with the new solo pilot of the Air Force Thunderbirds.

"So we did a little dance up and down the hall.

"And that's what it meant to us," he finished, "to have the burning desire satisfied. It was quite an experience!"

14

The Highest Praise

When the big blue mail distribution truck at Nellis Air
Force Base makes its daily rounds, it always stops and
brings a stack of letters to the Thunderbird office. Many
of these are from high-ranking Air Force officers, mayors
of cities, governors of states, and officials of other countries. But the letters the Thunderbirds best like to receive
are those from boys and girls all over the world.

The Thunderbirds have become world renowned by
taking their famous red-white-and-blue star-spangled jets
to nearly every country in the free world. They made
their first trip out of the United States in January 1954,
when they took the extensive goodwill tour of Central
and South America. More than three million people,
many of them seeing a jet airplane for the first time,
watched the team perform in eleven different countries.

A second tour of South America was made in November of 1957, marking the first appearance of truly super-

sonic aircraft on that continent. More than four million spectators watched the Thunderbirds perform at Buenos Aires, Argentina; Montevideo, Uruguay; and Rio de Janeiro, Brazil. The Presidents of Argentina and Brazil became the first heads of state to exceed the speed of sound when they were flown through the sonic boom barrier in a two-seated F-100F by members of the Thunderbird team. In March 1958, the team returned to the West Coast of South America for missions over the Panama Canal and at Lima, Peru. It was in 1958 that the Thunderbirds were presented with the Air Force Outstanding Unit Award by the Secretary of the Air Force for "exceptionally meritorious service of great national significance." This is the highest peacetime award given to a unit of the Air Force for outstanding service and achievement.

In 1959 the team went to the Far East for the first time. The team made its third tour of South and Central America in the fall of 1961. Long Legs Two, as the task force was called, visited sixteen countries, performing before 6,786,500 people. More than two milion spectators watched the team perform in Rio de Janeiro alone.

Capacity crowds were in attendance in all of the twenty-eight aerial demonstrations during this tour. At many of the show sites, officials said the team drew the largest audience ever assembled in their cities.

In the spring of 1963, the team made its first visit to the European continent. The Thunderbirds performed twenty-one aerial demonstrations in twenty-five days in the Azores, England, France, Germany, Italy, Spain, Luxembourg, and Libya. More than two million saw the Air Force's team during this tour, dubbed "Project Grand Play." The highlight of the trip was the Thunderbirds'

The Thunderbirds honor the plane's manufacturer as the red-white-and-blue F-100 Super Sabres make a flat pass over the North American Aviation company's chalet at the Paris Air Show in June 1967. *Courtesy U.S. Air Force*

appearance at the International Air Salon at Le Bourget Aerodrome, Paris, when they represented the United States in this important international exhibition of air power. Later in 1963, the team was awarded the first Oak-Leaf Cluster to the Air Force Outstanding Unit Award for exceptionally meritorious service of national and international significance.

The Thunderbirds set a new record by performing twenty-one demonstrations in twenty-three countries in 1965. "Operation Island Tide," a Caribbean jaunt, began the season in March; Europe was covered in June and July in "Operation Big Wing"; while "Operation Easy

A Thunderbird pilot greets a fan. *Courtesy U.S. Air Force*

Road" in November and December took the team to seven Latin American nations.

At the close of 1965, the Thunderbirds had performed as Ambassadors in Blue before more than sixty million spectators in forty-five countries.

Not all of these millions of people, of course, write to tell the Thunderbirds how much they enjoyed the show. But many boys and girls have written some interesting letters to the team members. The Thunderbirds say it's

The Highest Praise   135

the highest praise because it is for the boys and girls of the world that they give their most enjoyable performances.

Here are what some of the children have written after seeing the Thunderbirds:

Las Vegas, Nevada

The class thanks you for all you did. You didn't have to do all of this. It was really thrilling to see the Thunderbirds.

As we saw the Thunderbirds it gave us a feeling of safety and freedom. As the Thunderbirds passed over us, we saw that we were safe. I'm glad I'm an American because I know I'm free. There are men that are very young that are dead. They died for their country.

We also thank you for taking time to show the film about the Thunderbirds. Thank you very much.

Papendrecht, Holland

I am a Dutch boy of eight years old and I take a great interest in war planes, especially in stunt teams and I think that your team is one of the mightiest.

My older brother writes this letter for me, because I am not able to write English.

Here with I would kindly request you to send me photographs of your fabulous stunt team.

Thank you in advance! With kind regards from Holland, from the land of mills and clogs.

Great Falls, Montana

Dear Major Paul A. Kauttu,

While you were in Great Falls with the Thunderbirds, I watched both of your air shows. Boy, you're the neatest!!! It was a wonderful show!!!

Major, my parents asked me what I would like for my 10th birthday, March 15. Would it be possible to have a model of

the Super Sabre jet? I have $1.62 saved which I will send you and they said they would give a little more if it costs more. Would you please let me know if you can send it, and I will send you my money.
Thank you.
P.S. My mom copied my letter cause I'm kind of messy at writing.

Corpus Christi, Texas

Gentlemen—

I wrote you some time back about a colored picture of your group and forgot to put in my address to you so I my doing it now.

God bless you for the work you do, and the air show you do for us, and also God bless you and keep you safe in all your shows this year and in the years to come.

Limburg, Belgium

Dear Sir,

During the Airshow of June 27, 1965, which took place in Belgium at Brustem Air Force Base, the Belgium people could admire the fabulous "THUNDERBIRDS." Your team was just great! I never saw such risky and dangerous exercises! After the show I asked a friend for your address, and he gave me your Homebase-address, so that I could write a letter to you, to thank you for the beautiful demonstration you have given in Belgium.

I've always been interested in aerobatic teams, and now I dare ask You to send me some pictures of the famous THUNDERBIRDS, the US Air Force's official ambassadors in the air.

I will be pleased very well if You could send me the (perhaps colored) pictures of the team, with your signatures on a photograph.

I thank you in advance.

This lucky boy is realizing the dream of thousands of boys and girls who have seen the Thunderbirds. He has been chosen to don a pilot's helmet and climb into the cockpit of a Thunderbird F-100 Super Sabre. *Courtesy North American Aviation, Inc.*

Naranja, Florida

Dear Capt. Charles Hamm,

I saw the Thunderbirds in action. I like them very much. They were very good and no mistake was made in the air. I would see them a hundred times if I could. If you get a chance, would you send me some pictures of you and the Thunderbirds. Your admirer,

Denver, Colorado

Dear Sirs,

I'm very interested in the Tactical Air Command. I want to fly an F-105 "THUNDERCHIEF" more than anything in the world. I love the AIR FORCE but especially TAC. Here in Denver Colorado I've been to BUCKLEY AIR NATIONAL GUARD BASE and it's the neatest thing in the world. Those afterburners really shake you up. I have read that NELLIS AFB is the home for the "THUNDERBIRDS" too! I would appreciate it if you could send me some AIR FORCE AIR-CRAFT pictures. **THANK YOU**

Oklahoma City, Oklahoma

Dear Major Kauttu,

I want to thank you for sending me the picture. I got to see it for the first time this morning, as I have recently had eye surgery, as the result of an accident with a ball, and both eyes have been covered.

I hope to be able to see you and the Thunderbirds again sometime.

My best wishes for your continued success.
(by mother)

Amsterdam, Holland

Dear Sirs,

Having a hobby of aviation, of which I am very enthusiastic (my age is 16 years and I follow the classic high school), I collect photos of stunt-teams.

At first at home and later at school I have organized with some of my friends an exhibition on aviation and space-travel. I have received already several photos on the above mentioned subjects and have many books concerning them. A famous Dutch aviator opened the exhibition at school and was very fond of it. Within some time we hope to organize also an ex-

The Highest Praise   139

hibition in the Dutch Aviation Museum at Schiphol Airport. You would oblige me very much, by sending me some photos of the "Thunderbirds" in action, and a signed photo of the team, which will have a seat of honour at our next exhibition. Thanking you heartily in anticipation, I remain
Yours Sincerely.

New York State

I watched your air show at Niagara Falls last year. At the air show I had a stomach ache and was lying on my back watching the parachutists. But when you started your performance I had hardly noticed that I was standing up and feeling fine. The best cure for a stomach ache that I know of is the United States Air Force Thunderbirds.

Index

maneuvers, diamond, 42–49
maneuvers, solo, 54–62
Maracay, Venezuela, 20
Maultsby, Capt. Charles, 66, 73
Maxwell AFB, Alabama, 123–124
McChord AFB, Washington, 85
McCormick, Maj. Robert, 7
Mexico, 16, 18
Mexico City, 17, 18
Montevideo, Uruguay, 133
Myrtle Beach AFB, South Carolina, 24

Naranja, Florida, 138
Nellis AFB, Nevada, 13, 26, 33, 35, 66, 77, 86, 87, 103, 128, 130, 133, 139
Niagara Falls, New York, 140
Nicaragua, 16, 18
North American Aviation Corporation, 11, 81, 86

O'Donnell, Gen. Emmett, Jr., 67
Okinawa, 67, 68, 69
Oklahoma City, Oklahoma, 139
"Operation Big Wing," 134
"Operation Easy Road," 134
"Operation Island Tide," 134

P-47 Thunderbolt, 7, 79
Palmgren, Ed "Lucky," 63–64, 85, 103, 123–124
Panama, 16, 18, 133
Papendrecht, Holland, 136
Paris, 134
Patillo, Bill, 6, 20
Patillo, Buck, 6
Peru, 16, 18–19, 133
Philippines, 69
practice session, 24–26, 27–31, 35
"Project Grand Play," 133